Introduction – Suggestions for using this book

–

The Gifted Church

The Missional Church

The Ministry of All Christians

Suggestions for using this book

The vision of an "equipping church" in which all Christ followers are engaged in gifts-based ministry comes from Ephesians 4. This chapter begins with the Apostle, Paul, urging us to "lead a life worthy of the calling to which you have been called." That calling, which all of us share, is to follow Jesus, be his disciples, and join him in his ongoing work of ministry in the world. We are all endowed with spiritual gifts to do our part in a unified whole "for the work of ministry" and "for the building up of the body of Christ."

The writers of this devotional book are pastors who are part of congregations intentional about becoming every-member-in-ministry churches. We offer it to you as a source of encouragement, inspiration, and challenge to live day-to-day and moment-to-moment as ambassadors for Christ and ministers of the Gospel.

There are several ways to use this book:

✝ As a personal devotional guide for any 40-day period you may choose

✝ As a resource for a small discipleship group

✝ As a Lenten devotional guide – Start on Ash Wednesday and read through the meditations, skipping Sundays

✝ As a devotional guide during Advent

✝ As a congregation-wide focus on equipping ministry at wherever you are in the journey

✝ As part of your devotional time

✝ As readings chosen at random based on their thematic focus

—

Selections from *Meditations on the Ministry of All Christians* can be used in devotionals, in sermons, or in preparation for mission and service. We hope you find it helpful in your journey of deep discipleship and in the life of your congregation and small groups as they sojourn together as the Body of Christ, the Church.

—

Shared Ministry:
Examples from the Bible

—

THE MINISTRY OF ALL CHRISTIANS
Day 1
"God's Gifted People Are All Around You"

Exodus 18:13-26 (NRSV)

[13] The next day Moses sat as judge for the people, while the people stood around him from morning until evening. [14] When Moses' father-in-law saw all that he was doing for the people, he said, "What is this that you are doing for the people? Why do you sit alone, while all the people stand around you from morning until evening?" [15] Moses said to his father-in-law, "Because the people come to me to inquire of God. [16] When they have a dispute, they come to me and I decide between one person and another, and I make known to them the statutes and instructions of God." [17] Moses' father-in-law said to him, "What you are doing is not good. [18] You will surely wear yourself out, both you and these people with you. For the task is too heavy for you; you cannot do it alone. [19] Now listen to me. I will give you counsel, and God be with you! You should represent the people before God, and you should bring their cases before God; [20] teach them the statutes and instructions and make known to them the way they are to go and the things they are to do. [21] You should also look for able men among all the people, men who fear God, are trustworthy, and hate dishonest gain; set such men over them as officers over thousands, hundreds, fifties and tens. [22] Let them sit as judges for the people at all times; let them bring every important case to you, but decide every minor case themselves. So it will be easier for you, and they will bear the burden with you.

[23] If you do this, and God so commands you, then you will be able to endure, and all these people will go to their home in peace." [24] So Moses listened to his father-in-law and did all that he had said. [25] Moses chose able men from all Israel and appointed them as heads over the people, as officers over thousands, hundreds, fifties, and tens. [26] And they judged the people at all times; hard cases they brought to Moses, but any minor case they decided themselves.

> *Pastors end up taking on all kinds of roles and tasks, even if they're ill equipped to perform them, simply because they accept the understanding that "it's what they pay me for!" Meanwhile, laypeople sometimes shy away from ministry that they're well equipped to do simply because they're afraid they'll be stepping on the pastor's toes.*
>
> Sue Mallory, *The Equipping Church*

> *While laypeople feel underemployed, doing "busy work" in the church, pastors feel overemployed, trying to shoulder the impossible burden of being the minister of the church...We are convinced that the stagnation of the laity is caused by the frustrating power of a church system that keeps the laity marginalized and prevents the pastor doing the most important work: "equipping the laity for the work of the ministry." [Ephesians 4]*
>
> R. Paul Stevens and Phil Collins, *The Equipping Pastor*

—

Like so many pastors, Moses was trying to do it all.
Fortunately, Moses' father-in-law, Jethro, was there to
give him some good advice, *"You will surely wear
yourself out, both you and these people with you. For
the task is too heavy for you; you cannot do it alone."*
Jethro was a wise man. No one, not even a Moses
could do it all. Imagine what would have happened to
the Hebrew people if Moses had not listened. An
overworked, exhausted Moses could not guide God's
people out of the wilderness into the promised land. A
tired, overtaxed pastor cannot be a positive spiritual
force in a congregation.

Maybe you have heard of the 80:20 rule—the
situation in which 20 percent of the people do all the
work while 80 percent sit back and enjoy the benefits.
A community of faith, whether it's God's children in
the wilderness or in a local church, cannot move
forward with a sense of vision and purpose unless
everyone's gifts are recognized, cultivated and used
for the good of the whole. How effective can a church
or group be if one or two people are doing most of the
work? Unfortunately, too many pastors continue to
over function while their laity under function. It's not
a healthy situation.

As a pastor, I try to recognize the gifts of others and
to allow them to be in ministry within the body of
Christ, although sometimes I fall back into old habits
and forget that there are talented and gifted people all
around me willing to be equipped and released into
God's ministry.

—

One of my former churches decided that the Stephen Ministers—lay people who have received intense training as care givers and compassionate ministers in the church and community—would visit the hospitals on Mondays. I'll never forget the time I robbed a Stephen Minister of the opportunity to be in ministry. A church member was in a hospital some distance away. It was a Monday and a Stephen Minister was willing to make the trip to visit on behalf of the church family. I had a meeting near the hospital, so I called the Stephen Minister and told him that I would take care of the visit. It seemed like a good thing to do; there was no need for two people to drive the long distance. As I was driving to the hospital, it suddenly hit me that I had robbed a church member of a ministry opportunity.

I wonder how many times we, especially clergy, rob others of their opportunities for ministry. How often have we done something in the church that someone else is just as qualified to do? Without an every-member ministry, we fail to convey the biblical truth that God calls all people to a specific task within the body of Christ. When we purposefully and willingly do not allow others to be in ministry, we ignore the resources God gives the Church to transform people's lives, change the community and impact the world.

At the beginning of this forty-day journey, my prayer is for those of you who have tried to do it all. May you learn to give ministry away and to recognize the giftedness of God's people all around you.

—

For those of you who are still wondering about your place in the community of faith, my prayer is that you hear God's voice, because you are gifted; you are called to minister.

Get Equipped –
Be an Equipper

- **PRAY:** (Exodus 18:19) God goes before you. God will help you overcome your obstacles. Only God truly transforms our lives.

- **TEACH:** (Exodus 18:20) Hear the Good News. Teach the Good News. Remember, the goal of teaching and learning is personal transformation.

- **DELEGATE:** (Exodus 18:21-22) Commit to giving ministry away. There are other gifted people in God's Kingdom. Everything isn't dependent on you.

- **EQUIP:** (Exodus 18:21) You cannot do it by yourself. Find other gifted persons; pray with them, teach them if there is the need, and release them into ministry.

Prayer
Lord, help me to recognize the gifts of others and to understand that you have not called me to do it all.

NOTES:

THE MINISTRY OF ALL CHRISTIANS
Day 2
"There's Gold in the Pews"

Exodus 31:1-11 (NRSV)

[1] The LORD spoke to Moses: [2] See, I have called by name Bezalel son of Uri son of Hur, of the tribe of Judah: [3] and I have filled him with divine spirit, with ability, intelligence, and knowledge in every kind of craft, [4] to devise artistic designs, to work in gold, silver, and bronze, [5] in cutting stones for setting, and in carving wood, in every kind of craft. [6] Moreover, I have appointed with him Oholiab son of Ahisamach, of the tribe of Dan; and I have given skill to all the skillful, so that they may make all that I have commanded you: [7] the tent of meeting, and the ark of the covenant, and the mercy seat that is on it, and all the furnishings of the tent, [8] the table and its utensils, and the pure lamp stand with all its utensils, and the altar of incense, [9] and the altar of burnt offering with all its utensils, and the basin with its stand, [10] and the finely worked vestments, the holy vestments for the priest Aaron and the vestments of his sons, for their service as priests, [11] and the anointing oil and the fragrant incense for the holy place. They shall do just as I have commanded you.

> *If you want to build a ship, don't summon people to buy wood, prepare tools, distribute jobs, and organize the work, rather teach people the yearning for the wide, boundless ocean.*
> Antoine de Saint Exupéry

—

But, Mr., Ms. or Mrs. Layperson, I ask on the authority of the New Testament, have you forgotten who you are? You are a minister of Jesus Christ, a holy priest, an ambassador for Christ, an agent of reconciliation in the world, salt and light and yeast. You cannot assist your pastor. His job is to assist you in your ministry.

> R. Paul Stevens,
> *The Equipper's Guide to Every-Member Ministry*

God gave Moses, leader of the Israelites, the materials and measurements with which to build the Tabernacle; however, Moses did not have the skills for doing all of the work nor did God expect him to build it by himself. God intended for him to have plenty of help and told him that Bezalel, Oholiab and other craftsmen had the necessary skills. Moses supplied the materials and the information he was given and then let the gifted builders use their skills in ministry to accomplish the task of building the Tabernacle.

Our churches are full of gifted and talented people. There is gold in the pews! Unfortunately, we (the Church) often fail to mine and refine the precious gifts God has given every congregation. Christianity got its start and grew rapidly with the help of non-paid, faithful disciples of Jesus Christ. It was not until the late second century that church leadership became a day job that eventually led to a distinction between lay and clergy.

—

Today, Christianity thrives in places like China and Cuba, not because of the impact of professional clergy, but because of passionate and gifted laity. It's not my objective to lessen the important contributions of the clergy but to point out the important contributions of all of God's gifted people, both lay and clergy. We need each other! All of our gifts are essential for the ministry of our church as we endeavor to meet the challenges of being the Church in the twenty-first century.

It's a holy thing when a person discovers a passion for ministry and mission. Several years ago I took a group of people to a vision conference. They returned with a passion to bring the church to the surrounding community and decided to "Rock the Block" with the Good News of Jesus Christ. Every year that church invites the people of the surrounding community to the church grounds where they are greeted with Christian hospitality and opportunities to participate in a day of fun activities, free food, music, and free backpacks filled with school supplies for the children. It is the church's way of saying, "We are here and we care." One of the most successful ministry programs in the history of that church was generated by and is now guided and maintained by passionate and gifted laity. I'm convinced that if the clergy or the staff had stepped in to direct and guide the program, "Rock the Block" would not be as successful as it is.

—

Thousands upon thousands of untapped resources for the Kingdom sit in our pews each week. Ministry happens when gifted people realize they are ministers with gifts that can make a difference. The responsibility of the clergy and church professionals is to help God's people discover their gifts, to equip them for ministry, and then to release them into the world.

Mine it – Refine it

- **CALLED:** (Exodus 31:1-2) God doesn't just call ordained clergy. God calls all people to be in ministry. Have you ever heard God's call in your life? What was your response?

- **APPOINTED:** (Exodus 31:6-11) Hearing God's call and responding out of your giftedness allows you to be passionate about your work in the Kingdom and the Body of Christ. Have you found your place of ministry? Are your gifts being utilized in the Church, the Body of Christ?

- **FILLED WITH THE SPIRIT:** (Exodus 31:3) Deep in your heart there is an empty place waiting to be filled by the Spirit. Do you spend time in prayer asking for the Spirit's direction? Have you allowed the Spirit to help you identify your gifts for ministry? Are you passionate about your contribution to God's work?

___

- **GIFTED:** (Exodus 31:2) Filled with the Spirit you are able to share your gifts, your abilities, intelligence, and knowledge. Are your gifts recognized in the church? Have you participated in a gifts discovery process? Have you thought about how your gifts can best be used in the Church?

Prayer
Lord, Help me to recognize the giftedness of all God's people.

NOTES:

THE MINISTRY OF ALL CHRISTIANS
Day 3
"Teamwork is Healthy Work"

Exodus 35:30-36:7 (NRSV)

[30] Then Moses said to the Israelites: See, the LORD has called by name Bezalel son of Uri son of Hur, of the tribe of Judah; [31] he has filled him with divine spirit, with skill, intelligence, and knowledge in every kind of craft, [32] to devise artistic designs, to work in gold, silver, and bronze, [33] in cutting stones for setting, and in carving wood, in every kind of craft. [34] And he has inspired him to teach, both him and Oholiab son of Ahisamach, of the tribe of Dan. [35] He has filled them with skill to do every kind of work done by an artisan or by a designer or by an embroiderer in blue, purple, and crimson yarns, and in fine linen, or by a weaver—by any sort of artisan or skilled designer. [1] Bezalel and Oholiab and every skillful one to whom the LORD has given skill and understanding to know how to do any work in the construction of the sanctuary shall work in accordance with all that the LORD has commanded. [2] Moses then called Bezalel and Oholiab and every skillful one to whom the LORD had given skill, everyone whose heart was stirred to come to do the work; [3] and they received from Moses all the freewill offerings that the Israelites had brought for doing the work on the sanctuary. They still kept bringing him freewill offerings every morning, [4] so that all the artisans who were doing every sort of task on the sanctuary came, each from the task being performed, [5] and said to Moses, "The people are bringing much more than enough for doing the work that the LORD has commanded us to do."

———

[6] So Moses gave command, and word was proclaimed throughout the camp: "No man or woman is to make anything else as an offering for the sanctuary." So the people were restrained from bringing; [7] for what they had already brought was more than enough to do all the work.

> *The key to a winning team is not the head coach's play calling but instead his recruitment and selection of outstanding assistant coaches and players and letting them do their jobs.*
>   Bear Bryant

> *Healthy community and teams are built around the individuality of gifts, team accountability, and willingness of people to work for the good of the greater body.*
>   Sue Mallory, *The Equipping Church*

One person cannot carry the burden of decision-making nor of solving all the problems in a church. Moses found this out as he tried to make decisions and to settle all of the differences that inevitably arose among his people. After some coaching from Jethro, he learned to share the joy of ministry by seeking out and appointing gifted people to help him lead. He learned that when individuals come together with a passion for ministry, amazing things can happen.

—

A church is at its best when the gifts of its members are shared through teamwork. Often nominating committees go through the painful process of trying to come up with names to fill slots and many times end up "driving square pegs into round holes" just to get the job done. Teams, on the other hand, work best because they are not formed through such a system but by allowing persons to choose their areas of ministry based on their individual gifts and passions. Someone recently commented to me, "I know I don't come to Finance Committee meetings. I'm not even sure why I was nominated. Numbers and money are not my passion." Why do we do this to people when they can better serve the Kingdom by using their gifts and graces where they can produce healthy results?

We are all leaders with a responsibility to work together for the betterment of the whole, the Church. The process works best when we participate out of our giftedness rather than from a sense of obligation. Don is a good example of an individual who used his special gifts and passion to influence others to contribute their gifts for a worthy project within his church and community. He saw the need to provide an opportunity for all children and young people in the community to participate in Christian-based athletics. Others with the same interest joined Don to form an Upward team, and together they organized an Upward basketball program in the church's facilities. There, children can participate no matter what their skill level.

The program has expanded to include Upward basketball, soccer, and flag football. A partnership with another church now allows even more adults to find their places in ministry through Upward bound and it is making a monumental impact on families in the community. Don is so passionate about what he does that he spends many hours a week over and above his forty-hour-a-week job to coordinate Christian athletics in his community.

When people are guided through an effective gifts assessment and discipleship process, they find their way to a team. Working with a team allows them to share and express their passion in a productive and self-enriching way. There are others like Don who have found a place in ministry by regular attendance at team meetings and a passion for sharing their gifts. Think of other examples of how teamwork has produced healthy relationships, self-satisfaction and pride, and brought about healthy results within the community and its churches.

Discover your Passion
Find a Team

- **SKILLED:** (Exodus 35:30-33) Our skills are honored within the Body of Christ and are utilized there for mission and ministry. What skills do you bring to the Body of Christ? Does your church currently honor and value your God-given skills? If so, how?

- **PASSIONATE:** (Exodus 36:1-2) When you are passionate about God's calling, you look for ways to share your passion, to build up the Body of Christ and to make a difference in your community and the world. What is it that you enjoy doing more than anything else? Have you expressed your passion to someone in your church? How can the church help you find a place of ministry that is linked to your passion?

- **INVESTED:** (Exodus 36:3-5) People invest time, money and resources in those things about which they are passionate. Where and how do you invest your resources? Is there a direct correlation between how you use your resources and your passion? Have you ever considered becoming a team member for ministry? Does your church already have a team that you could join to use your gifts and graces in a helpful way?

- **MISSIONAL:** (Exodus 36:3-7) Sharing your skills, passions, investment of time, money and resources equals a mission that can change your life and the life of others. If you had an opportunity to do one thing that would positively impact the life of others, what would it be? How are you making a difference right now in your workplace, community, home, and church?

Prayer
Lord, guide me to the place where my gifts can best be used for the Body of Christ.

NOTES:

THE MINISTRY OF ALL CHRISTIANS
Day 4
"The Ministry of All God's People"

Acts 13:1-3 (NRSV)

[1] Now in the church at Antioch there were prophets and teachers: Barnabas, Simeon who was called Niger, Lucius of Cyrene, Manaen a member of the court of Herod the ruler, and Saul. [2] While they were worshiping the Lord and fasting, the Holy Spirit said, "Set apart for me Barnabas and Saul for the work to which I have called them." [3] Then after fasting and praying they laid their hands on them and sent them off.

You are a minister of Christ. In all fairness, an exposition of the ministry of the laity has to begin with that statement. If you are a baptized Christian, you are already a minister. Whether you are ordained or not is immaterial. No matter how you react, the statement remains true. You may be surprised, alarmed, pleased, antagonized, suspicious, acquiescent, scornful, or enraged. Nevertheless, you are a minister of Christ.
Francis O. Ayres

I guess my frustration is that I can't see anywhere in the Church a recognition of or much support for the only kind of ministry that I and most Christians can have--the daily plodding along wherever you are sort of thing. Trying to offer up whatever you do to God, rarely seeing how it could make much difference.

> *I've come to think of it as an invisible ministry because it's invisible not only to the world, but even to yourself most of the time. It's a difficult kind of ministry at best, but more so because generally it isn't even seen as a valid ministry at all, or at least that's my impression.*
>
> A Lay Person to Her Bishop

Imagine for a few minutes what the world would be like if God's people saw themselves as ministers seven days a week in their homes, in their workplaces, and in their places of play and leisure. What it would be like if the Church, in a visible and significant way, recognized the ministry of all persons, lay and clergy. Imagine the impact if all of God's people were sent into the world with the confidence and understanding that they are ministers as their paid pastors are! It's time for clergy and church staff to let go of the trained-expert-called-to-do-it-all mentality.

It's time for the Church to change its focus and stop saying to people "I need you to do this," or "Would you do that?" It's time for the Church to listen to its people and to say, "How can I help you discover your gifts, equip you and release you into ministry? When a person is approved as a candidate for ministry, those present at the meeting often lay hands on and pray for the candidate.

—

The time has come for the Church to do the same for its people—to recognize the giftedness of the people who sit in worship, who sing in choirs and play in praise bands, who teach Sunday school, usher, and participate in the business of their church. It's time for the church to say, "Tell us how we can help you and we will pray for you and will do all we can to equip you, a person of God, and then will release you into ministry."

This approach raises up ministers instead of creating reluctant volunteers. Which do you think God prefers?

The twenty-first century Barnabases, Sauls, Simeons, Luciuses, and Manaens are sitting in our pews. They are waiting to hear God's call. They are waiting for us to lay our hands on them, to pray for them, and to release them into ministry. It's a new day, and the Church is poised to be a tremendous force in our world through the ministry of all of God's baptized people.

Called, Equipped, Released

- **CALLED:** (Acts 13:2) All baptized Christians are called to be in ministry. Have you heard God calling you? Do you feel like a volunteer or a minister? Have you let your church know about your special calling? How can the church support you as you answer your call to ministry?

- **LIFTED UP IN PRAYER:** (Acts 13:3) The Body of Christ must pray for its ministers, both clergy and lay. Has your church prayed for your call and ministry? How would it make you feel if you knew your church and its people are praying for you as you walk the path of discovery and ministry?

- **RELEASED:** (Acts 13:3) All of God's ministers are challenged to be the Church, not just on Sunday, but on Monday through Saturday as well. What difference would it make if the Church recognized your ministry at home, in the work place, or in some other important part of your life?

Prayer
God help me to recognize the ministry of all people and to celebrate your work through all others in the community and world.

—

THE MINISTRY OF ALL CHRISTIANS
Day 5
"A Gifted Body"

Romans 12:3-8 (The Message)

³ I'm speaking to you out of deep gratitude for all which God has given me, and especially as I have responsibilities in relation to you. Living then, as every one of you does, in pure grace, it's important that you not misinterpret yourselves as people who are bringing this goodness to God. No, God brings it all to you. The only accurate way to understand ourselves is by what God is and by what he does for us, not by what we are and what we do for him. ⁴⁻⁶ In this way we are like the various parts of a human body. Each part gets its meaning from the body as a whole, not the other way around. The body we're talking about is Christ's body of chosen people. Each of us finds our meaning and function as a part of his body. But as a chopped-off finger or cut-off toe we wouldn't amount to much, would we? So since we find ourselves fashioned into all these excellently formed and marvelously functioning parts in Christ's body, let's just go ahead and be what we were made to be, without enviously or pridefully comparing ourselves with each other, or trying to be something we aren't.

⁶⁻⁸ If you preach, just preach God's Message, nothing else; if you help, just help, don't take over; if you teach, stick to your teaching; if you give encouraging guidance, be careful that you don't get bossy; if you're put in charge, don't manipulate; if you're called to give aid to people in distress, keep your eyes open and be quick to respond;

—

if you work with the disadvantaged, don't let yourself get irritated with them or depressed by them. Keep a smile on your face.

> *Above all the grace and the gifts that Christ gives to his beloved is that of overcoming self.*
> Francis of Assisi

> *Spiritual gifts are the power of the Holy Spirit flowing through you to impact others.*
> Unknown

During the last several decades, a wealth of resources have been developed to support teaching and training on spiritual gifts in the local congregation. Spiritual gifts inventories abound - assessments designed to assist an individual in discerning his/her giftedness. Indeed, a gifts discovery process is an integral component of any equipping church. Because of this emphasis on individual gifts discovery, it's easy to think of spiritual gifts as an individual matter. Nothing could be farther from the truth. The Scriptures bear witness that spiritual gifts are a corporate phenomenon. God gives gifts to the Body of Christ, and intends that gifts be exercised in community.

Romans 12:3 (NIV) reads, "For by the grace given me I say to every one of you: Do not think of yourself more highly than you ought, but rather think of yourself with sober judgment."

—

This passage is reminiscent of Philippians 2:1-4, "If you have any encouragement from being united with Christ . . . then make my joy complete by being like-minded, having the same love, being one in spirit and purpose. Do nothing out of selfish ambition or vain conceit, but in humility consider others better than yourselves. Each of you should look not only to your own interests but also to the interests of others."

We think of ourselves more highly than we ought when we privatize spiritual gifts. An emphasis on the gifts of the individual reduces spiritual gifts to a commodity, a possession to be used at one's own discretion. The focus is on us, the individual, not on our Great God, the Lord, the Giver of good gifts, and not on our gifting for the Body. While we all acknowledge that it is God who gives spiritual gifts, it's easy to receive the gift from God's hand and then effectively take it out of God's hands. In this deception, God is still Giver, but when a person receives the gift as "possession" the control of its exercise lies with the individual. This privatized control and exercise of gifts is not God's design. A more faithful response to God's gifting is to make oneself and one's gifts available at God's discretion in concert with others and their gifts. In the words of John Wesley's Covenant Prayer, "let me be employed for you or put aside for you."

God designed the Church to be the Body of Christ. This image affords us not only a beautiful and descriptive metaphor for our life together, but radically, and in the mystery of the Gospel, we ARE the Body of our risen Lord here on earth.

—

God has ordained and established that each and every believer is a functional member of this massive corporate Body! If spiritual giftedness were an individualized or privatized matter, we'd have individual "toes," "eyes," "spleens," "elbows," "ears," "thumbs" all running around the world trying to perform their function disconnected from the Body!

This passage in Romans 12 and the wonderful passage on gifts in 1 Corinthians 12-14 demonstrate that God gives spiritual gifts to the Body of Christ through individual members. Spiritual gifts are given to the Body; spiritual gifts are given through (not TO) individuals. This distinction must be grasped in order for a Body of Believers to thrive and become healthy. God does indeed gift individuals. Gifted individuals are placed in the Body as channels of God's grace as part of a corporate expression of God's love and goodness.

In a thriving Body, each member performs a God-given function. Each member understands their vital role in the community. Each member lives and moves and has being as a channel of God's grace - that essential conduit through which flows the giftedness God gives to the Body. No one is off the hook; no one remains passive; no one is considered "less than;" no one is considered "more than;" no one is overlooked.

—

Continuing to lift up the corporate nature of spiritual giftedness, we will help the members of our congregations understand that performing their function in the Body is as natural and as necessary as the functioning of their own organ systems in their own bodies. Keeping the focus on the corporate nature also prevents individuals from wrongly believing that they have nothing to offer (no giftings) or from shelving their "tools" and choosing not to utilize them. A healthy Body runs autonomically as God's Holy Spirit continually breathes life and bestows gifts. Hallelujah!

God Gives Spiritual Gifts TO the Body of Christ through Individual Members

- **GOD:** (Romans 12:3) God is the Giver of gifts. Spend time today thanking God for bringing giftedness to the Body of Christ through YOU.

- **INQUIRE:** (Romans12:3-5) Spend time in prayer inquiring of God about your attitude and opinions around spiritual giftedness. Ask God to illumine your thoughts and motivations. In what ways do you feel insecure or unworthy, in what ways have you coveted others' giftings, in what ways do you feel complacent, in what ways do you feel over-confident?

- **FIND:** (Romans 12:6-8) Find out what spiritual gifts you bring to the Body of Christ. Ask your pastor or a member of your church's Equipping Team for a good spiritual gifts inventory, and then talk with someone about your findings after you complete the survey. Then find a way to begin serving as a channel of God's grace and gifting in or through your local Body.

- **TEACH:** (Romans 12:3-8; 1 Cor. 12) Seek out ways to teach others about spiritual giftedness and the Body metaphor from scripture. Encourage your leaders to teach and preach regularly on these important biblical truths.

Prayer
Lord, thank you that you give gifts to the Body of Christ through individuals like me. Show me the role that I'm to play in your Body, and help me to exercise that function in the grace you continuously provide.

—

THE MINISTRY OF ALL CHRISTIANS
Day 6
"Gift Your Gift!"

1 Peter 4:10-11 (ESV)
[10] As each has received a gift, use it to serve one another, as good stewards of God's varied grace:
[11] whoever speaks, as one who speaks oracles of God; whoever serves, as one who serves by the strength that God supplies—in order that in everything God may be glorified through Jesus Christ. To him belong glory and dominion forever and ever. Amen.

> *God wants you! Are you hearing me? What God wants in ALL of you. He wants to consume you. In that process you will serve. Service is good, but your service won't count for much of it if it isn't done with a giving of self, with a yielding of your inner person and all that you are about. That's what God calls us to; a life of giving of ourselves.*
> John Wimber

> *God doesn't call the qualified; God qualifies the called.*
> Unknown

Yesterday, in our reading from Romans 12, we reflected on the communal nature of the Church. Because we are the Body of Christ, each member is inter-connected. God doesn't give gifts to people in isolation. God gives gifts to the Body through gifted individuals to edify and complete the whole. Just as a healthy toe can't help but perform its function in the body, so healthy believers can't help but perform their individual roles in the Body of Christ.

—

Today, our text reminds us that indeed we are gifted members, and the exercise of our giftedness is a component of our stewardship.

To be a disciple of our Lord Jesus Christ is to be a good steward. Our text invites us to be good stewards of the manifold grace of God! God showers grace upon us in abundant and marvelous ways. Within that grace-shower are gifts, spiritual gifts, which God rains down freely upon his people. The terms "grace" and "gift" are intimately related in scripture. God graces us with spiritual gifts and as we exercise them, we return the gift to God out of love, adoration, and gratitude. The exercise of our giftedness brings God glory as we become channels of God's grace to a lost and hurting world.

Our text tells us that we minister God's grace as we serve in our giftedness. Many churches have adopted the mantra "Every Member a Minister," and that's a true statement! Every believer is called to be a minister by virtue of his or her baptism. Anyone who calls upon the Name of Jesus walks in a divine calling to minister God's grace in its various forms. Each of us has a vital role to play. The Body is impoverished if any part is missing; we are not to neglect our gifts or to miss opportunities to steward our giftedness well.

It's astonishing how many people in the pews of our churches across the United States have no idea that they're spiritually gifted! It's heartbreaking to ask the question to a gathered Body, "how many of you have a spiritual gift?" and to see very few hands raised around the sanctuary.

—

We have a responsibility as leaders to impart the gift to our people that they are gifted! Preaching and teaching on spiritual gifts and exhorting our people is a gift in and of itself. Our text is clear, "as each has received a gift" - each person has received a gift. Each one!

No one is exempt because the grace of God is abundant and exuberant and manifold! When God bestows grace and hands out gifts, no one is left out. Sadly, people place themselves in the "scratch and dent" section of our sanctuaries - this is an artificial holding area that simply does not exist scripturally. Let's speak words of life to our Bodies - rebuke the lie that people have been deceived into believing, the lie that says "I'm not gifted; I have nothing of value to offer" - and call people forth into the light of grace and truth; into the freedom and joy that comes from walking in giftedness, fueled by the strength of God's grace.

Embrace Your Giftedness
Steward Your Gift

- **PONDER:** Do you believe that you are spiritually gifted? Why or why not?

- **PRAY:** Ask God to speak to you about your spiritual giftedness. Ask God to name the gift(s) that He has graciously bestowed through you. Thank God for His grace.

- **DECLARE:** Making declarations from God's Word is a powerfully formative exercise. Throughout this day, declare the following statement out loud: "I have been given a spiritual gift. I will steward it well with the strength God provides." (1 Peter 4:10,11)

- **WALK:** Ephesians 2:10 declares that you are God's workmanship - God's masterpiece - created in Christ Jesus to do good works, which God prepared in advance that you might walk in them. Take a new step today in exercising your giftedness for the sake of God's Kingdom.

Prayer
God, thank you for giving me a spiritual gift. Help me to steward it well and minister faithfully to others so that you may receive glory and praise. Amen!

THE MINISTRY OF ALL CHRISTIANS
Day 7
"We are Connected"

John 15:1-5 (NRSV)
[1] "I am the true vine, and my Father is the vinegrower.
[2] He removes every branch in me that bears no fruit.
Every branch that bears fruit he prunes to make it
bear more fruit. [3] You have already been cleansed by
the word that I have spoken to you. [4] Abide in me as I
abide in you. Just as the branch cannot bear fruit by
itself unless it abides in the vine, neither can you
unless you abide in me. [5] I am the vine, you are the
branches. Those who abide in me and I in them bear
much fruit, because apart from me you can do
nothing.

> *I was born to a woman I never knew, and
> raised by another who took in orphans. I do
> not know my background, my lineage, my
> biological or cultural heritage. But when I
> meet someone new, I treat them with respect.
> For after all, they could be my people.*
> James Michener

> *In an industrial culture tired of "punching in"
> and a technocratic culture desperate to get
> "plugged-in" (but plugging in to all the wrong
> energy outlets), followers of Christ connect
> people to the many positive sources of energy-
> -from the sun to the soul--but especially to the
> most powerful energy source in the universe:
> Jesus Christ!*
> Leonard Sweet, *Quantum Spirituality*

———

I recently visited a vineyard in the county where I live. As I admired the perfectly straight rows of vines, I noticed a sign attached to one of the long trellises that read, "First vines planted in 1976." My guess is that many of the vines in the vineyard had their start with those first plantings. Cuttings were brought from other vineyards and grafted onto the vines to start new varieties; to make stronger, healthier and more disease resistant vines; and to increase the vineyard's production and longevity.

As I admired the long, straight rows of vines; I couldn't help but think of Jesus' image of the vine in the Gospel of John and our connection to God through Jesus Christ. The Body of Christ grows through our connection to one another and to God through Jesus. Christ is the vine and when we graft ourselves to Him we not only bring love and grace into our lives but into the lives of others.

Someone commented that the Church isn't much different from most of our civic organizations. "The Rotarians, Lions, and Civitans have fellowship and a sense of civic responsibility. They have different forms of outreach and help thousands of people. In many cases, they have a real sense of community within their organizations. So, what makes the Church different?" he asked." My immediate response was "Jesus Christ is the difference."

—

We are a community of faith, a collection of branches, connected to Christ the Vine. We need each other. Someone once said, "I can't be me without you." We cannot be who we were truly created to be without each other and without Jesus Christ. Vineyard owners will tell you that the strongest point on any vine is the place where the vine and the branch are joined. Likewise, it is at the point where we are connected to Christ that we are the strongest. That connection makes the Christian community unique, for it is what brings us together as a community of faith and makes us strong so that we can produce fruit worthy of the Kingdom of God.

Your Connection to Christ

- **CHECK YOUR CONNECTIONS:** Your strongest points are those places where you are connected to Christ. Where do you connect to Christ in your life? Do you sense that your connections to Christ are strong?

- **CONNECT TO CHRISTIAN COMMUNITY:** Your connection to Christ also brings you into a community of followers of Christ where love and grace can be shared and received. Where do you connect to other followers of Jesus?

- **CONNECT TO PURPOSE WITH PURPOSE:** Your connection with Christ and other followers helps you to grow spiritually? Are you growing in your relationship with Christ and with others? What changes do you

———

need to make in your life in order to graft yourself more fully into Christ?

Prayer

Lord, help me connect to you more fully and to grow in my relationship with others.

—

NOTES:

The Ephesians 4 Church

THE MINISTRY OF ALL CHRISTIANS
Day 8
"When the Lord Calls"

Ephesians 4:1-3 (NRSV)
[1] I therefore, the prisoner in the Lord, beg you to lead a life worthy of the calling to which you have been called, [2] with all humility and gentleness, with patience, bearing with one another in love, [3] making every effort to maintain the unity of the Spirit in the bond of peace.

> *What is the center of your passion and giftedness? You need to be able to put your finger on it.*
> Michael Slaughter, *Unlearning Church*

> *Each member of the people of God stands under God's call. Each is accountable to God for his or her response to it. Ministry is rooted in a prior call of God upon every believer.*
> Greg Ogden, *The New Reformation*

I left my cell phone at home the other day and drove back four miles to retrieve it. Our phones have become an extension of our bodies. We think we cannot live without them and we would not dare try. One of the things I've learned after thirty years of ministry is that there is a difference between good and important. It might be a good thing for us always to be available; on the other hand, is every phone call important? I don't think so!

We are called by God and that's a good thing. That call is not only good, but it is the most important call you'll ever get. Unfortunately, God's call doesn't get the same priority as many of our daily calls on the cell phone. God needs every one of us to be an active part of the Body of Christ and to consider His call a priority. You are a minister and God is calling you. He wants you to answer His call by putting your gifts and passion to a worthwhile use.

In today's scripture, Paul describes a worthy life. Each of us is called to be a part of the Body. The Body works best when each of us approaches our ministry with humility, gentleness, and patience. He says that we are to respect other's contributions and gifts. He challenges us to love even when we disagree or are frustrated by others. A unity of spirit exists when we are all respectful of everyone's contributions and gifts.

One of my favorite stories is told by the author Nikos Kazantzakis. A young man went in search of a famous monk. When he finally found the monk, he asked him, "Father Makarios, do you still wrestle with the devil?" "Not any longer, my child; I have grown old and he has grown old with me. He does not have the strength. I now wrestle with God." "With God!" exclaimed the young man in astonishment. "And you hope to win?" "No," answered the monk. "I hope to lose."

We often struggle with our call from God as we try to interpret it for our lives. God works hard to spend time with his gifted children and wants to help us find our way in the world.

—

God is eager to communicate with us and to provide support and guidance throughout our life journey. By answering God's call, you allow Him to be the winner in your struggle with Him. We all have a place in the Body of Christ. Can you ignore a call like that?

You are Worthy

- **WORTHINESS:** (Ephesians 4:1) Are there times when you sense a call from God but feel you are not worthy to answer that call? Do you feel that you are in a wrestling match with God because of your lack of confidence in yourself? Are you willing to lead a life worthy of God's calling? Remember, God calls YOU. YOU ARE WORTHY!

- **LOVE:** (Ephesians 4:2) Loving is often very difficult, but Paul tells us to lift up all of God's people in love. Do you sense God's love flowing through others in the Body of Christ? Do you let the love of God flow through you to others?

- **UNITY:** (Ephesians 4:3) Unity doesn't mean that we always have to agree but that we understand the importance and purpose of our ministry. We cannot meet the challenges of God's Kingdom work unless we can come together as one body. What does it mean for us as members of the Body to disagree but to still have unity within the Body? When is disagreement destructive? When can it be helpful? What is your church's unity of purpose?

- **PEACE:** (Ephesians 4:3) God wants peace in the world, in our homes, and in our churches. Why is peace so important? What destroys peace in the Body of Christ? What is the relationship between unity and peace? Are you at peace with others, with God and with yourself?

Prayer
Lord, help me to know that I am one of your unique children. Please make your presence known as I respond to your call as a worthy member of the Body of Christ.

—

THE MINISTRY OF ALL CHRISTIANS
Day 9
"One in Christ"

Ephesians 4:4-6 (NRSV)

[4] There is one body and one Spirit, just as you were called to the one hope of your calling, [5] one Lord, one faith, one baptism, [6] one God and Father of all, who is above all and through all and in all.

> *The body of Christ is the last place on earth where people do their own thing. Christbody connections are where duty to other is ascendant over duty to self, where the gifts of the Spirit are used for the upbuilding of the community and not for the self. The church is a divine creation, an organism of which one is a living 'member,' that lives the life of Christ and incarnates, however imperfectly, Christ's real presence in the world.*
> Leonard Sweet, *Quantum Spirituality*

There's an old saying that goes something like this: "If you ever meet anybody who thinks like you do, you're lucky; if you ever meet two, you're blessed. You'll never meet three." God created a beautiful and blessed diversity of people in the world and in the Church. However, one body, does not mean conformity. Oneness in Christ does not mean sameness. When the Apostle Paul talks about "one body" and "one spirit," he does not mean a "cookie-cutter" mentality.

The Church, the Body of Christ, is not in the business of cloning, of making Christians who look, act, and respond the same. We cannot all have the same gifts and graces. "One body" and "one spirit" doesn't mean sameness. Churches that insist on uniformity, who parrot the same jargon and move lockstep in a prescribed theological rhythm do the Body of Christ a great injustice.

The great historian, author and Christian, C.S. Lewis, says some important things about the Church, one of which relates to Paul's understanding of the Church, the Body of Christ. He says that the model too many of us have in mind for the Church is the same model we have for secular organizations—just another group we join. Then we do what members of an organization do—we go to the meetings and pay dues. However, this was not Paul's understanding of the Body of Christ. He believed that God's people should be joined to his Church in the same way that the members of the physical body are joined to a body. It is a living relationship. The Body of Christ gives life to its members and they, in turn, are indispensable to the Body. When God's diverse and gifted people join hands in ministry and mission, they are able to make a tremendous difference in the world.

—

Several years ago about a little boy who wondered from his South Dakota home. When the parents couldn't find him, the police were called. They organized the Boy Scouts, neighbors and others into a search party. For three days hundreds of people moved through the prairie hoping to find the little boy before he succumbed to the elements. On the morning of the forth day, one of the searchers suggested they get organized. "Let's join hands, form a line, and sweep up and down the prairie until we find the boy.

They formed a line a quarter of a mile long, making an impressive sight as they moved across the prairie holding hands. On the third sweep, they found the boy lying dead in a small ditch behind some brush where he had apparently tried to protect himself during the cold prairie nights. Gently they carried the boy's body to his waiting mother. When they put the boy in her arms, there was complete silence, then the distraught mother looked up and said, "Why didn't you join hands sooner? Why didn't you join hands sooner?"

Members of the Body of Christ must join hands sooner rather than later and recognize the giftedness of all its members. God's people must come together in one body and one spirit so that the entire world might know of God's great love. Let no one say, "We should have come together sooner."

—

One Body, One Spirit

- **CALLED TO BE PART OF THE BODY:**
  (Ephesians 4:4) God has equipped and gifted
  each of us as a part of the Body of Christ. Do
  you have a sense of your unique place within
  the Body of Christ? How does the Body of
  Christ encourage your spiritual growth and
  ministry? Do you do your part to use your
  unique gifts as a member of the Body of
  Christ?

- **GOD OF ALL:** (Ephesians 4:5-6) All of
  God's people are baptized into one baptism.
  We are one faith and there is one God of us
  all. What is your understanding of one
  Baptism yet many people?

Prayer
*Lord, help me to see my baptism and oneness within
the Body of Christ as a unique part of your ministry
in the world.*

THE MINISTRY OF ALL CHRISTIANS
Day 10
"The Measure of a Gift"

Ephesians 4:7 (NRSV)
[7] But each of us was given grace according to the measure of Christ's gift.

> *A saint is not someone who is good but who experiences the goodness of God.*
> Thomas Merton

> *The child of God knows that the graced life calls him or her to live on a cold and windy mountain, not on the flattened plain of reasonable, middle-of-the-road religion.*
> Brennan Manning
> *The Ragamuffin Gospel*

I worked at a sporting goods store during my sophomore year in High School. One of my jobs was stringing tennis rackets. The higher end racquets were shipped to the store without strings allowing tennis players to customize their strings and tension. I was the "go-to guy" to help tennis players get the custom racquet of their dreams. It was the mid seventies and the wood racquet was being replaced by metal, aluminum, and fiberglass. Players like Jimmy Connors and Arthur Ashe were shaking up the tennis world with their strange new racquets and style of play. Then in 1975, Ashe changed the tennis world forever by becoming the first African American to win Wimbledon by defeating Connors.

—

At the time, I did not comprehend or really pay attention to that remarkable feat. He broke the color barrier in tennis, but it wasn't easy. He endured racist's remarks, taunts, double standards and all manner of hatred and ugliness. He coped with his situation by playing championship tennis and maintained his integrity by taking the higher path as a follower of Jesus Christ. He inspired others to do the same. Ashe wrote in his autobiography:

"If I had one last wish before I die, I would ask that all Americans could see themselves as one, past the barbed-wire fences of race and color. We are weaker for these divisions, and the stronger when we transcend them. We must reach out our hand and heart in friendship and dignity both to those who would befriend us and to those who would be our enemy."[1]

With great grace, Arthur Ashe used his God-given gift to make a difference in the tennis world. His influence is still felt today. Like Ashe, we have received grace according to Christ's gift. Our influence and contribution to the Body of Christ is just as important as Ashe's gift to the tennis world.

The Measure of Your Gift

- **GOD IN YOUR LIFE:** (Ephesians 4:7) God's grace is not limited nor is it reserved for just a few. Where do you see God's grace in your life? Where does God's grace reveal itself to you within the Body of Christ?

---

[1] *Days of Grace*, (written with Arnold Rampersad)

- **GRACE AND GIFT:** (Ephesians 4:7) Your giftedness comes from God. How are you using and honoring God's gifts in your life?

Prayer

Lord of all creation, thank you for your grace and for the gifts I am able to share in the Body of Christ. Help me to recognize other's God-given gifts.

NOTES:

THE MINISTRY OF ALL CHRISTIANS
Day 11
"Supporting Roles"

Acts 6:1-7 (NRSV)

[1] Now during those days, when the disciples were increasing in number, the Hellenists complained against the Hebrews because their widows were being neglected in the daily distribution of food. [2] And the twelve called together the whole community of the disciples and said, "It is not right that we should neglect the word of God in order to wait on tables. [3] Therefore, friends, select from among yourselves seven men of good standing, full of the Spirit and of wisdom, whom we may appoint to this task, [4] while we, for our part, will devote ourselves to prayer and to serving the word." [5] What they said pleased the whole community, and they chose Stephen, a man full of faith and the Holy Spirit, together with Philip, Prochorus, Nicanor, Timon, Parmenas, and Nicolaus, a proselyte of Antioch. [6] They had these men stand before the apostles, who prayed and laid their hands on them. [7] The word of God continued to spread; the number of the disciples increased greatly in Jerusalem, and a great many of the priests became obedient to the faith.

> *Help, I need somebody, help, not just anybody, help, you know I need someone, help.*
> Paul McCartney and John Lennon

Steve spent a week in the Gulf immediately after hurricane Katrina. While there, he had the opportunity to help the disaster relief coordinator for the Mississippi Annual Conference of the United Methodist Church and his wife. The couple, who usually helped others, found themselves the victims of a natural disaster and needed help themselves. Steve and others tried their best to help the couple rescue what they could from their house that was still filled with four feet of water. Unfortunately, the government closed down the neighborhood and stopped all cleanup efforts because of the sewage, bio-hazards, and petroleum products in the water, preventing them from accomplishing their task. It was a sad and difficult situation. As they prepared to leave the scene, the pastor/disaster relief coordinator said, "All of my ministry I have tried my best to help others. This is the first time in my life I've been on the receiving end. You've come to me in my helplessness to bring help. Thank you."

In today's passage from Acts, the Apostles are concerned that they are neglecting their responsibility as prophets and preachers of The Word. The widows need food, but the Apostles need help in order to provide their needs. As representatives of their church, they recognize the importance of spreading God's word and of their Christian responsibility to the widows. They call a meeting and seven are appointed to look after food distribution. The scripture tells us, "The word of God continued to spread; the number of the disciples increased greatly in Jerusalem, and a great many of the priests became obedient to the faith."

Here we see the early Church working through the needs of the Christian community in a healthy and productive way. The Church is at its best when gifted people share in the responsibilities of ministry and service. It's not the flamboyant who make the world go around. It's those who work quietly and faithfully in the service of Jesus Christ. The Apostles were the early leaders of the Church, but they could not have succeeded without the help of others in supporting roles. It takes all of God's gifted servants to make the Kingdom work. What would Moses have done without Aaron? Would there have been a King Saul or David without the support of Samuel who anointed them to the task? Would the Apostle Peter have survived without his brother Andrew working in the shadows? What about Barnabas, who quietly ministered at the side of Paul? We all need help, even the pastors among us.

Your Supporting Roles

- **TAKE STOCK:** What supporting roles do you perform in your home, church, or community?

- **EVALUATE:** How do your supporting roles help grow and expand God's Kingdom work?

- **REMEMBER:** When have you been a recipient of the service of others? What did it feel like to be on the receiving end of service?

- **LOOK AROUND:** Who needs your help and support? Go to them and offer yourself, your time, your encouragement, your gifts, your resources, and your abilities.

Prayer
O God, help me to identify those places where I can play a supporting role in your Kingdom. Help me to be receptive to your strength and grace as I support others and also when I receive their support.

THE MINISTRY OF ALL CHRISTIANS
Day 12
"When the Church is Healthy, She Dances!"

Ephesians 4:11-13 (The Message)
He handed out gifts above and below, filled heaven with his gifts, filled earth with his gifts. He handed out gifts of apostle, prophet, evangelist, and pastor-teacher to train Christ's followers in skilled servant work, working within Christ's body, the church, until we're all moving rhythmically and easily with each other, efficient and graceful in response to God's Son, fully mature adults, fully developed within and without, fully alive like Christ.

> *When the Church is healthy, she dances!*
> Sue Mallory

> *Dance, then, wherever you may be. "I am the Lord of the Dance," said He.*
> From the song, "Lord of the Dance"

Jesus Christ our Risen Lord and Savior ascended to the right hand of the Father in order that we might have life and have it abundantly. Because Christ reigns eternally from this heavenly position, Christ established His Church to be His Body here on earth - carrying on His ministry until He returns. The Holy Spirit breathes life into this Body, filling and fueling it with everything we need for health and vitality. God's design and intent is that we would be a healthy Body - vibrant and alive, dynamic and rhythmic, fluid and flexible.

Picture a gymnast, an acrobat, a ballet dancer - all of these gifted athletes depict dynamic rhythmicity. This is the picture that the Apostle Paul paints for us in today's text in his description of Christ's Body.

The Message translation captures this metaphor with poetic beauty, "moving rhythmically and easily with each other, efficient and graceful in response to God's Son, fully mature adults, fully developed within and without, fully alive like Christ." What a stunning depiction of what it means to be a Body of Believers! Rhythmic, efficient, graceful, fully alive - these are the adjectives by which God longs to describe your local congregation. According to the Word, this is God's design for the Church - a Body, fully alive. So how do we get there?

A healthy Body is established by the equipping of the saints. Our text tells us that it was Christ Himself who gifted the Church with particular types of leaders (apostles, prophets, evangelists, pastors, and teachers,) and charged those leaders with the responsibility of preparing God's people for works of service - equipping the saints for the work of the ministry. The result of this equipping of the folks is a healthy, vibrant Body. Our text bears witness to this reality and calls us forth toward its realization. God does not intend that the leaders take sole responsibility for the ministry and merely enlist God's people to "help." God intends that leaders equip God's people to walk in their giftedness, to fulfill their God-given role as a member of the Body of Christ (Romans 12, 1 Corinthians 12).

The word that is translated in Eph. 4:12 as "equip," "prepare," or "perfect" depending on your translation, literally means "to mend/prepare fishing nets." As a fisherman "equips" his nets, he restores them to their intended purpose; he readies them for usefulness and functionality. As leaders equip God's people, they help to make the people ready to embrace their calling and to walk in their purpose and destiny. God does not desire that Christian leaders be "doers of all significant things;" God requires that Christian leaders be equippers of the saints.

Our local congregations will become healthier Bodies as pastors and people, leaders and laity begin partnering together in ministry, becoming intentional and purposeful about equipping the saints for the work of the ministry.

Equip the Saints – Learn to Dance

- **EXAMINE:** Take a look at your local congregation. To what extent do the leaders (pastors, staff, key leaders) understand themselves to be Equippers? Is the culture of your congregation one of "every member in ministry?" Does your church have systems and processes in place to help people connect with gifts-based ministry?

- **PROCESS:** Make an appointment to process the questions above with your pastor and other key leaders.

- **DANCE:** As you examine and process, paint a picture (metaphorically or actually/visually!) of what your congregation would look like as an "Ephesians 4:13 Dancing Body."

- **PLAN:** Develop three to five steps that your leaders can take to guide your congregation toward more fully becoming an Equipping Church.

Prayer

Lord Jesus Christ, I praise You for giving leaders to Your Church and for charging them with the privilege and honor of equipping Your people for works of service. Help us, by your grace, to fulfill this calling with integrity and faithfulness in my local congregation. Amen!

THE MINISTRY OF ALL CHRISTIANS
Day 13
"Going on to Maturity"

Ephesians 4:14-15 (NIV)

[14] Then we will no longer be infants, tossed back and forth by the waves, and blown here and there by every wind of teaching and by the cunning and craftiness of men in their deceitful scheming. [15] Instead, speaking the truth in love, we will in all things grow up into him who is the Head, that is, Christ.

> *When I was young I was sure of everything; in a few years, having been mistaken a thousand times, I was not half so sure of most things as I was before; at present, I am hardly sure of anything but what God has revealed to me.*
> John Wesley

If you've ever spent time at the beach, you will no doubt have passed some hours watching children play in the ocean's waves. Little heads bobbing up and down with each passing wave; small bodies pushed to the sand in the shallows under the influence of the breakers; diminutive figures in the chaos of the deep being pushed hither and yon under the watchful eye of lifeguard and parent. Today's text is puzzling at first glance, because the Apostle Paul seems to mix his metaphors. First, we're engaged with the Body of Christ, then the focus shifts to small children tossed by waves.

There is, however, consistency in Paul's message. Just as an immature body cannot long endure the fury of the ocean's waves, an immature Body cannot withstand the pressure of the world and systemic forces (waves) that would seek to combat it from all sides. Christ declared that He would establish His Church and the gates of hell will not prevail against it (Matthew 16:18). Such a Church is a strong, vibrant, resilient Body. It is the Church of Ephesians 4:13 and 16. Paul steps back for a moment in verse 14 to emphasize his point. A mature, healthy Body has grown beyond infancy; it is able to stand strong and persevere. No longer a small child bobbing on a turbulent sea, this Body is more like an Olympic swimmer or a triathlete pressing forward with determination, measured stroke by strong, measured stroke.

This fortified Body matures in Christ, Who is the Head. We are, after all, Christ's Body, and we must not lose sight of the fact that Christ Himself is the Head - the vital control center of the central nervous system. Connected to our Head, Who is Truth, we maintain ourselves by speaking truth in love with the members of this maturing Body. Truth and Love become a sustaining force, helping the Body persevere through the tumultuous waters of life. This Body grows and matures as each member fulfills its function - just as our human bodies grow and mature as each organ system completely develops toward full functioning. Part of our truth speaking must involve exhorting our members to assume their appointed place in the Body of Christ - to participate actively in the maturation and healthy functioning of the community.

The "Dancing Church" of Ephesians 4:13 is the "Olympic Swimmer Church" of Ephesians 4:15. Both images remind us that God's design is that His Church would be a strong, dynamic, rhythmic, and persevering Body. God's leaders must continually lift up this metaphor and never give up on summoning God's people to fulfill their role and function in this vibrant, life-giving Body.

No Prolonged Infancy –
Growing Up in Christ

- **PONDER:** What factors contribute to churches remaining spiritual "infants?"

- **PRAY:** Ask God to show you areas in which your congregation has been held back in spiritual infancy. Ask God for wisdom and discernment that you might speak into these areas with love and grace.

- **DECLARE:** Making declarations from God's Word is a powerfully formative exercise. Declarations actually pave the way for God's Word to be realized and embodied in your life and ministry. Spend time this week declaring over your congregation, "speaking the truth in love, we will in all things grow up into him who is the Head, that is, Christ." (Eph. 4:15)

Prayer

Creator God, just as you've designed babies to grow up and become adults, so you've designed your Church to grow to maturity in Christ, Who is our Head. By your grace, help my congregation to become a healthy, mature Body.
Amen!

THE MINISTRY OF ALL CHRISTIANS
Day 14
"Fitted Together for Service"

Ephesians 4:16 (NLT)
He makes the whole body fit together perfectly. As
each part does its own special work, it helps the other
parts grow, so that the whole body is healthy and
growing and full of love.

> *Connection happens when we place the right*
> *people in the right places for the right reasons*
> *at the right time.*
> Bruce Bugbee

> *The kind of work God usually calls you to is*
> *the kind of work (a) that you need most to do*
> *and (b) that the world most needs to have*
> *done . . . The place God calls you to is the*
> *place where your deep gladness and the*
> *world's deep hunger meet.*
> Frederick Buechner,
> *A Theological ABC*

The ministry of "connections" is a vital component of
any equipping church, yet sadly it is often the weakest
link in an otherwise sound system. Self-discovery,
ministry matching and placement reside at the heart
of ministry connections. Strong equipping churches
develop simple systems wherein intentional
conversations take place all the time with people in
the congregation.

—

These conversations afford the opportunity to gather all kinds of information - people's stories, their hopes and dreams, their "highs and hurts," their experiences, their spiritual giftedness, their personality type, their talents and abilities, their passions, their sense of purpose, their dreams and destinies. Connection happens when we take all the information that we've gleaned about our people and the needs of our congregation and our community and begin to fit them together. The work of Connections Ministry is not unlike assembling a jigsaw puzzle. At first, you may find yourself staring at a lot of individual pieces, not knowing where to begin, but over time, as you develop intentional plans and systems for putting the pieces together, you'll find that a beautiful picture begins to emerge.

Using scripture's metaphor of the Body, think about Connections Ministry as the "tendons and ligaments." Ligaments and tendons connect various parts of the body into the whole. Imagine a human body that was missing its tendons and ligaments - it would not be able to function, because there wouldn't be anything connecting the muscles to the skeleton. You'd have a functional skeletal system and strong, sturdy muscles, but the body would be immobilized. So it is with our churches, our local Body of Christ, if the connections are missing.

—

When you develop a Connections Ministry in your local congregation, you must maintain a Kingdom focus. Ministry in, through, and to your local community and beyond is essential and non-negotiable for Equipping Churches. Your church cannot contain all the giftedness that God has poured out by His grace. Some people in your congregation have a specific calling that fits them well to serve inside the church; others have a calling to serve outside the church in the wider community. A strong Connections Ministry helps people connect with "the place where [their] deep gladness and the world's deep hunger meet," as Frederick Buechner said so well. Part of being an Ephesians 4 Equipping Leader is helping folks "find their fit" - either serving in the church or serving out in the world. Research conducted by Leadership Training Network revealed that a church that has fully mobilized her people will usually see 50% of the people serving inside the church walls and 50% serving outside in the community (*The Equipping Church*, Sue Mallory, pg 136).

A strong Connections Ministry involves helping people maintain their first point of connection - worshipping God together corporately - and then connecting with a way to give/serve and also with a way to receive and be nurtured in the Body of Christ. Connections Ministry fosters holistic discipleship - worshipping, serving, and being nurtured in the faith.

Well Connected – Find Your Fit

- **LOOK AROUND:** How easy is it for a person to get connected to a place to serve in or through your local Body? How easy is it for a person to get connected to a place to be served/nurtured in your local Body?

- **THINK SYSTEMS:** What are some simple steps you can take in your local Body to develop the "tendons and ligaments" of a Connections Ministry?

- **ACT:** Together with your pastor and a few key leaders, implement some measurable steps to develop those tendons and ligaments.

Prayer

God, I marvel at how you created Your Church to be a healthy Body. Help us to bring the tendons and ligaments to life in our local Body so that all God's people can find their fit. Amen!

NOTES:

The Equipping Leader

THE MINISTRY OF ALL CHRISTIANS
Day 15
"Who's In Charge, Here?

Ephesians 4: 15-16 (NRSV)

[15] But speaking the truth in love, we must grow up in every way into him who is the head, into Christ, [16] from whom the whole body, joined and knit together by every ligament with which it is equipped, as each part is working properly, promotes the body's growth in building itself up in love.

> *Is the love of God shed abroad in your heart?*
> *Do you desire nothing but Him? Is He your*
> *glory, your delight, your crown of rejoicing?*
> *Do you love every person, even your enemies,*
> *as Christ loves you and gave himself for you?*
> *Do you desire to please him in all things?*
> *Have you intended to devote all your words*
> *and works, your business, studies, [and]*
> *diversions to His glory?"*
> John Wesley

The "center" of equipping ministry is discipleship. And the center of discipleship is Jesus. As part of equipping churches we see ourselves as fellow followers in a "followship" of co-ministers and co-missioners. We are co-learners and cojourners on the way of discipleship, the way of Jesus. As the role of pastors and staff shift from service providers to ministry coaches and equippers, helping more Jesus followers into the work of ministry, some may ask, "Who's in charge, here?" Jesus is the head of the Church. Jesus is in charge here.

Len Sweet, in his book *I Am a Follower*, asserts that movement toward Christ is not about leadership, but about followship. "The church is not led by leaders but by Christ. The head of the church is Christ. Everyone else is a follower. He's convinced that focusing on what we call leadership "has led us to a place where everybody is trying to get everybody else to do something…" What we are learning is that equipping ministry is not about filling slots on committees or recruiting people to keep church programs going. It's about deeper discipleship that produces a deep desire to serve Jesus, as Jesus serves.

When I was hiring and mentoring young adults to work on the various ministry staffs at Lake Junaluska Assembly, a United Methodist conference and retreat center, I told them, "If you need me to keep you on task and direct your work, I have hired the wrong person. We are all motivated by the love of Christ, all responding to the call of Christ. Let the mission, his mission, drive you, direct you, and empower you." A passionate preoccupation with Jesus defines and directs every action, every affection, and every desire of those who love him. For the Christ-Follower:

> The answer to who is Jesus
> The answer to what is Jesus
> The answer to why is Jesus
> The answer to how is Jesus
> The answer to when is now.

Only when Christ is the head of each and of all will we be joined and knit together by every ligament with which it is equipped, as each part is working properly, promotes the body's growth in building itself up in love.

John Wesley called for a kind of group discernment and decision making that he described as "holy conferencing." This kind of decision making is ruled by Jesus, not Sir Robert (of *Robert's Rules of Order*). Communities of faithful followers are prompted by the movement of the Holy Spirit, not motions from the floor. In this manner of governance, we seek not merely what appears to be the best alternative between a few choices, but the way of Christ according to his example of love, namely, love of God and love of neighbor.

Do things Jesus' Way

- **SURRENDER** all illusions of power and control and in its place sow humility and faith. Replace the need to be right with the desire to be righteous.

- **BE STILL** and know God. Cultivate an inner sanctuary that is free of anxiousness, fear, and restlessness.

- **DISCERN** the will of God after the heart of Jesus against the standard of love of God and neighbor and the heart prayer, "thy kingdom come on earth as it is in heaven."

- **FOLLOW** the counsel and the leading of the Holy Spirit as you follow Jesus into God's preferred future for the world, for the church, and for you.

Prayer
Gracious Lord, help me begin every decision-making process with an undeniable sense of your presence.

THE MINISTRY OF ALL CHRISTIANS
Day 16
"Sustainability: Ministry for the Long Haul"

John 15:1-8 (NIV)
[1] "I am the true vine, and my Father is the gardener. [2] He cuts off every branch in me that bears no fruit, while every branch that does bear fruit he prunes[a] so that it will be even more fruitful. [3] You are already clean because of the word I have spoken to you. [4] Remain in me, and I will remain in you. No branch can bear fruit by itself; it must remain in the vine. Neither can you bear fruit unless you remain in me. [5] "I am the vine; you are the branches. If a man remains in me and I in him, he will bear much fruit; apart from me you can do nothing. [6] If anyone does not remain in me, he is like a branch that is thrown away and withers; such branches are picked up, thrown into the fire and burned. [7] If you remain in me and my words remain in you, ask whatever you wish, and it will be given you. [8] This is to my Father's glory, that you bear much fruit, showing yourselves to be my disciples.

> *Solitude begins with a time and a place for God, and God alone. If we really believe not only that God exists but also that God is actively present in our lives-- healing, teaching and guiding-- we need to set aside a time and space to give God our undivided attention.*
>
> Henri Nouwen

Take heart that God prunes fruitful vines. If you've ever experienced pain, frustration, or disappointment in the midst of God's pruning, then find comfort in these verses. God prunes the fruitful vines – not the unfruitful ones – in order that they might grow to greater fruitfulness, ultimately for God's glory. Our Heavenly Father is a loving Gardener. God's work of pruning is a loving act – nurturing, caring, delighting – in a very intentional and deliberate manner. As we abide in Christ, we avail ourselves to God's delighting in us as He shapes us for His purposes.

God prunes the branches that abide. It's glaringly obvious that a branch removed from the vine cannot bear fruit. It's not only obvious – it's ludicrous to imagine that it could produce fruit! How could a branch that is cut off from its life source possibly thrive? And yet if we're honest, most of us live much of life working really hard to be fruitful in our own strength and limited resources. Why do we so often choose to become lifeless, dry and brittle (disconnected) when we have been given the gift of God in Christ to abide in the Vine and be fruitful?

As related in our text, Christ makes the disciple's role and task crystal clear: the disciple is to abide. The term "abide/remain" and its antithesis, "apart," occur six times in this short text, which serves to underscore and emphasize the directive. The Greek term that is translated "remain," or "abide" carries a sense of permanence. When one abides, she does not come and go – she dwells permanently.

—

As Christians, we often fail to assume residence in the Vine; or we live and behave as if we were somehow disconnected from our Life Source. Our permanent dwelling place is in Christ the Vine.

Startlingly enough, the disciple is not summoned first to action, but is called to abide. Out of the abiding, flows the fruitfulness! The problem with discipleship in many of our churches is that well-intentioned leaders exhort the people to live faithfully – to keep commandments and to exercise spiritual disciplines and to give generously and to serve sacrificially – but these leaders neglect to encourage the people that all such obedience is possible only if they first, foremost, and forever abide in Christ in order to receive his life and energy. Sincere leaders often set the folks up to become "dead branches" and then expect them to bear fruit! Ironically, these "dead branches" may in fact be good "church people."

Good "church people" serve on committees, appear overtly pious, faithfully attend worship, participate in Sunday School or Bible study, give tithes and offerings – all "good" deeds for sure, and not without merit. However, when we exhort faithful "doing" out of obedience to Christ, we often set people up to live in fear and guilt because they fail to measure up to the high bars we set. Or, we set them up to falsely and smugly trust in external religiosity, a contemporary pharisaical legalism. A critical question becomes, how can we, as leaders, equip people to become disciples, rather than to be good church people? The solution begins by exhorting people to abide first and allow Christ to fuel and direct the doing.

In a similar vein, leaders desire to be servants, but they wind up tired and frustrated, dried up and withered, because they miss the good news that fruitfulness comes from abiding. Or, leaders may become deceived into believing that their production equals true fruitfulness. Just as a branch needs the nutrients of its vine, so do we find our source of strength and energy by abiding in Christ and feasting on His Word. Any leader of integrity desires to bear good fruit for God's Kingdom. We work hard at fruitfulness, expending great energy and personal sacrifice. God promises fruitfulness to those who abide in Christ.

Just as discipleship cannot be attained by striving, one does not arrive at Equipping Leadership by "trying harder." Freedom and fullness in discipleship and leadership comes through abiding in the Vine and being continually filled with Living Water. A vibrant and fruitful ministry flows out of "being," not out of "doing." The posture of abiding sets a person up for a lifetime of freedom and fulfillment in life and ministry.

(Adapted with permission from The *Serving Leader for the People of God*, Elizabeth Wourms and John Stahl-Wert, The Ship Company, 2011)

Abiding in the Vine – Sustained for the Long Haul

- **REFLECT:** In your mind, what is the difference between a "church member" and a "disciple," between a "church leader" and an "equipping leader"?

—

- **ACT:** Engage people on your team or in your sphere of influence in conversation about these differences. Together, identify ways to help the people in your congregation develop disciplines of abiding.

- **REFLECT:** Name the distractions and/or obstacles that prevent you from abiding in the Vine.

- **ACT:** Write down two actions that you can take immediately to eliminate the distractions and obstacles that keep you from abiding in Christ.

Prayer
Lord Jesus, You are the true Vine! Help me to always abide in you so that I can bear fruit for your Kingdom. Amen!

NOTES:

THE MINISTRY OF ALL CHRISTIANS
Day 17
"Ministry as Coaching – Coaching as Ministry"

1 Thessalonians 2:11-12, 5:11 (NIV)
^{2:11} For you know that we dealt with each of you as a father deals with his own children, ¹²encouraging, comforting and urging you to live lives worthy of God, who calls you into his kingdom and glory . . .
^{5:11} Therefore encourage one another and build each other up, just as in fact you are doing.

Hebrews 3:13 (NIV) But encourage one another daily, as long as it is called Today, so that none of you may be hardened by sin's deceitfulness.

2 Corinthians 1:3-5 (NIV) ³ Praise be to the God and Father of our Lord Jesus Christ, the Father of compassion and the God of all comfort, ⁴ who comforts us in all our troubles, so that we can comfort those in any trouble with the comfort we ourselves have received from God. ⁵ For just as the sufferings of Christ flow over into our lives, so also through Christ our comfort overflows.

> "If you hear a voice within you say 'you cannot paint,' then by all means paint, and that voice will be silenced."
>
> Vincent Van Gogh

The term "coaching" brings many images to mind, and indeed we experience many types of coaches in our everyday lives. Sports coaches, life coaches, executive coaches, debate coaches . . . the list is nearly endless.

—

When we speak of coaching as ministry, we're referring specifically to participating in the work of the Holy Spirit as comforter, exhorter, encourager for the People of God; and in helping to release the God-given potential in other people. Chris Hardy and Elizabeth Wourms developed a working definition of "ministry coach" during an Equipping Leader class series they taught at United Theological Seminary. A ministry coach is "A catalyst along the journey of discovery and purpose for the individual and the team." This coaching role is not only for leaders in the church - God invites all believers to be encouragers and exhorters for one another.

In the scripture passages referenced above, the key verbs - encouraging, comforting, urging - all derive from the same word. It's the Greek word from which we get the term ascribed to the Holy Spirit, the *Paraklete*. Just as the Holy Spirit is our Comforter, our Encourager, we too are called by God to fulfill that role with one another.

Coaching as ministry becomes not so much about coaching for performance, but rather coaching for potential. God invites us to mine the gold that He has placed inside each person formed in His image and to release that potential for Kingdom purposes. As we comfort, encourage, and urge one another higher and farther, we become catalysts for the release of the purpose and destiny that God has placed in the hearts of His people. The ultimate goal of ministry coaching is to contribute to transformation of people with whom the coach is in relationship, so they effectively develop into healthy and whole people.

—

God invites us to come alongside one another and walk together - helping one another to shoulder burdens, carry concerns; to inspire one another to press on and persevere; and also to celebrate successes and joys along the way.

Coaches provide a supportive structure of concern, support, and planning - all of that can be summed up as encouragement. In everyday practice, this supportive environment includes things like affirmation, recognition, and other forms of support such as celebration, planning, problem-solving, redirecting, and providing resources. Affirmation is celebrating someone for who they are; recognition is celebrating someone for what they've done or accomplished. Both actions are vitally important to encourage the hearts of our people. Equipping Leaders - Coaches - constantly affirm and recognize the folks with whom they serve in ministry. Coaches offer continual support to those around them in helping to develop goals and plans, assisting with problem solving, and providing needed resources or counsel. It's all about being available and intentional to walk with the people with whom you're in ministry.

People-development is the highest calling of ministry leaders. Coaches are more concerned with the growth and discipleship of the people around them than with the work that gets accomplished. Obviously the work is vitally important, but the first priority is the development of the people whom God has called into the work.

—

Coaching is all about disciple-formation. Coaches provide the space for people to grow both as a disciple through their service and to be effective and efficient in ministry. We serve our people well as we help them become intentional about their own growth and development and also to develop intentional plans and processes for the ministry that they're involved in.

The ultimate goal of ministry coaching is transformation. As coaches - encouragers, exhorters, comforters - we play a catalytic role in the discipleship of other people. Imagine yourself as such a coach, contributing to the development of healthy, mature, and effective people. What a glorious calling! We are each called to play that role - disciples making disciples. This is not a role reserved for leaders in the church; God calls all of us to participate in the transformative work of the Holy Spirit in calling us as believers higher and farther along our journey in Christ.

Be an Encourager!

- **ENCOURAGE:** Hebrews 3:13 exhorts us to encourage one another daily. Name some specific ways that you can encourage the people on your team, committee, staff, group, or the congregation at large. Begin offering daily encouragement to people - mark your calendar so you remember!

- **BE CREATIVE:** Brainstorm some specific ways that you can recognize and celebrate people for what they're doing in ministry in your congregation. These ideas could involve

---

small gifts, writing notes of gratitude or encouragement, celebrating birthdays, celebrating key accomplishments, recognizing folks during corporate worship - the possibilities are endless!

- **ACT** Put your ideas into practice - begin regularly affirming and recognizing the people around you.

Prayer

God, I marvel at how you created Your Church to be a healthy Body. Help us to bring the tendons and ligaments to life in our local Body so that all God's people can find their fit. Amen!

NOTES:

THE MINISTRY OF ALL CHRISTIANS
Day 18
"Decreasing and Increasing"

John 3:27-28, 30 (NRSV)

[27] John answered, "No one can receive anything except what has been given from heaven. [28] You yourselves are my witnesses that I said, 'I am not the Messiah, but I have been sent ahead of him.'...[30] He must increase, but I must decrease."

> *Being a part of success is more important than being personally indispensable.*
> Pat Riley

> *I hope the term "the equipping pastor" is not an oxymoron. There is a lot of talk about equipping. But is it happening? When I went to seminary, I was taught to be a deliverer of service. All of the really great role models I knew were champions at delivering service. They spent countless hours laboring in ministry. But they did the ministry alone. That was what they were being paid to do. Some pastors keep ministry to themselves because of insecurity. They think if they do all the work, they will be indispensable and the church could never get rid of them. Someone said, "The indispensable person ought to be dispensed with immediately." It does take a self-confident, inspired pastor to embark on this kind of ministry of lay training.*
> James W. Moss, Sr.[2]

---

[2]http://www.newlifeministries-nlm.org/people/7-20_Equipping_for_Service.htm

---

There was a movie a few years ago called *Failure to Launch* about a 30-something young man who was still living with his parents. His mother still cooked his meals and did his laundry, and his dad did all of the bread winning and bill paying. Of course, the man/boy did anything his parents asked him to do to help out, but he didn't take responsibility for much. They made it easy for their immature son to continue living as a dependent child, and yet, they longed for him to grow up, find a job, sustain a relationship, get married, and move out! On the one hand, they wanted their son to grow up and go about his life, but on the other hand, they liked being needed.

The same kind of thing can happen in the church as the average church member allows the clergy and ministry staff to be the "real" ministers. The paid staff may grumble a bit about the challenge of getting church folks to "support the church's ministries," but the arrangement provides job security and role identity for the ministry staff and clergy and a "representative ministry" for church members. The goals of equipping ministry are to help every member mature as a Christian disciple and to assume their own spirit-gifted ministry, "moving out" into the community as a minister of the Gospel.

The long-standing traditional role of the clergy and ministry staff must decrease so the role and ministry of member-ministers may increase. It's going to take some soul searching, some habit breaking, and some role changing to get there. Maybe not so much "decrease" as radically change:

—

- From doing to teaching.
- From taking responsibility to increasing the response-ability of others.
- From providing ministry services to helping member-ministers be in ministry.
- From being up front to being behind the scenes.
- From a ministry directed by designated religious professionals (DRPs) to one directed by the Holy Spirit and enacted by the whole people of God.
- From a hierarchy of titles to partners in ministries.
- From deferring to clergy to deferring to Jesus and deferring to one another according to our gifts, experience, and roles. Sue Mallory says you can get a good idea about the culture of a church by which direction heads turn when a question is asked in a meeting. Our pooled experience, insight, and faith are far greater than that of any one pastor or staff member.

Cleaning up our language
The pop music group, *The BeeGees* reminds us, "it's only words, but words are all I have, to steal your heart away." It will take a change of vocabulary fueled by a deep sense of calling and love for Jesus, and for the Church, to move us beyond the distinction between clergy and laity. That unbiblical divide hampers spirit-gifted every-member-ministry. It will help us in our mission to be the church if we start with the way we use the word "church."

When we say we are "going to church" we do much damage to our mission and our ecclesiology. It turns us inward, toward a specific location. We are the church, the aggregation of all Christians. If we are the church, wherever we are, *there* is the church!

And how about the word "minister?" All who follow Jesus are ministers, called to do the things he does. All of us have been endowed with spiritual gifts "for the work of ministry (Ephesians 4:12). I am a pastor. All of us are ministers. Let's abandon the language of "volunteers" who do what they can to support the mission of some organization or group and adopt the language of ministers who are called and equipped to be the church.

Four Phases of Ease

David Stone, youth ministry guru and cable television pioneer came up with a process of handing off ministry to church members that he called "The Four Phases of Ease." It puts into action the notion of one person's role decreasing as another person becomes more competent and confident in that same role. It progresses through these phases:

- I do and you watch (and learn)
- I do and you do (we do it together sharing and sometimes echoing roles)
- You do and I watch (I'm still here if you need me, but you take the lead)
- You do and I move on to something else ("You've got this!")

Some ministry staff may have mistakenly described this process as "working their way out of a job!" The fact is, it is their job. I've heard some clergy colleagues say, "What's my role, then? If I loose my identity as THE minister, who am I in the church?" Elton Trueblood offers this answer:

> The ministry is for all who are called
> to share in Christ's life, the *pastorate*
> is for those who possess the particular
> gift of being able to help other men
> and women to practice any ministry
> to which they are called." The
> equipping pastor initiates the
> maturing of the body by assisting the
> people of God to practice the
> ministries to which they are called.

One indicator of progress in becoming an equipping church is the degree to which church people see themselves and each other as "ministers."

- **REFLECT:** Take a shot at filling in these blanks: I have a ministry of _____ to/with/for _____.

- **DISCERN:** In what specific ways are you trying to hold onto a staff-driven and pastor-centered church culture?

- **BE HONEST:** What threatens, offends, or confuses you about seeing yourself and your fellow church members as "ministers?"

—

- **CHANGE YOUR LANGUAGE:** Give yourself six weeks of referring to your pastor as something else besides "the minister." That's your title or definitive name in the body of Christ.

Prayer
Gracious God, help me remember that I am a minister of the Gospel in every sphere of life. Amen.

—

THE MINISTRY OF ALL CHRISTIANS
Day 19
"Releasing Ourselves for Ministry"

Mark 6:7 (NRSV)
[7]He called the twelve and began to send them out two by two, and gave them authority over the unclean spirits.

Luke 10:1-2 (NRSV)
[1]After this, the Lord appointed seventy others and sent them on ahead of him in pairs to every town and place where he himself intended to go. [2]He said to them, "The harvest is plentiful, but the laborers are few; therefore ask the Lord of the harvest to send out laborers into his harvest.

1 Corinthians 5:20a (NRSV)
[20]So we are ambassadors for Christ, since God is making his appeal through us…

> *Equipping ministry is less a program of the church than it is a new way of being the church. It is a way that takes seriously the gathering of the church for worship and education, but also the scattering of the church for ministry in daily life.*
> The Empowering Church

> *Courage is not the absence of fear. It is the conviction that something is more important than fear.*
> - sign on a coffeehouse wall

Jesus says we are the salt of the earth. Here's an acrostic on the word "salt" that may help us remain salty and useful, and may help release us for active ministry, both as individuals called by Christ himself and as congregations called to be his body.

SALT:
See the needs around you
Ask for partners, not permission
Love God and neighbor
Thresholds – cross the lines, move through the barriers, get off your "buts" and claim the power of the Holy Spirit and the promised presence of Christ, and take the next step!

Seeing

When I was growing up, my mother used to say that I suffered from selective seeing. "Don't you see the clothes on the floor?" "Don't you see the dishes in the sink?" I guess I just looked past them. I knew if I saw them I'd have to do something about them! Seeing with the eyes of Christ means that we will see the people in need around us. We will see when the "way things are" needs to change to the "way God intends them to be." That's when "somebody oughta" turns into, "I'm gonna."

Ask for Partners, Not Permission

You don't have to ask for permission or get approval to do the work of Christ. You have his permission, even his commission.

—

If someone asks, "By what authority are you doing this?" as some asked Jesus and his original disciples, take advantage of this teachable moment to explain that you are a duly ordained minister of the church, by your baptism, your spiritual gifting, and by the call of Jesus. The authority of your missional activity will be judged to the extent that it embodies Jesus, here and now, to the extent that you are indeed doing the things he does. An equipping church culture takes seriously each disciple's gifts and calling to do the work of Jesus in the world with passion and purpose. We have so many potential partners in this holy work.

Love God by Loving Neighbor
This will actually help with the seeing part, and the crossing thresholds part, too. When the Pharisees asked Jesus to select the one greatest commandment in the Law, answered with two; love God and love neighbor. Jesus understands that these two are inseparable if either is to be fulfilled. To fulfill the law of God, you can't merely adore or revere God. You have to love your neighbor as well. John Wesley asserts that being religious and keeping holy habits such as regular worship attendance, Bible study, and personal prayer only gets you halfway there. He calls this kind of personal piety, "almost Christian." The love of God has to extend to love of neighbor, especially those deemed as the least among us, for it to be complete. Jesus goes so far as to say, "Whatever you do for the least of these, my brethren, you do it to me."

———

Cross Thresholds

Everybody has experienced some kind of threshold moment – that first kiss, speaking up when it would have been easier to keep quiet, taking or leaving a job, or literally crossing the threshold of an unfamiliar place. "Crossing the line" is generally considered an unwise thing to do, but Jesus calls us to cross the thresholds of fear, social etiquette, and cultural divides to join him in his ministry. Trade in your WWJD bracelet for one that asks WIJD, "What is Jesus doing?" Find out what Jesus is doing and join him there. "For most of us, what will be required to engage in missional Christianity is simply to reach out beyond our fears and ignorance of others to overcome our middle-class penchant for safety, to take a risk and get involved in what God is already doing in our cities and neighborhoods."[3]

Apostolic Succession

Jesus has a system for keeping his ministry movement going and growing. Jesus chose 12. Then he chose 70 more. And they all went out, baptizing and teaching, passing the mantle of ministry from one disciple to another. This mantle passing continues to this day, not only from ordained clergy to lay folk, but from follower/disciple to follower/disciple. Alan Hirsch, in his book *Here and Now*, describes our common task as "activating the whole people of God and empowering every believer to be active agents of God's kingdom in every sphere of life.

---

[3] Alan Hirsch and Lance Ford, *Right Here, Right Now* (e-book location 468-475)

The Jesus Formula for every-member ministry goes like this:

> Come and see.
> Abide in me.
> Be me.

The Church needs to understand itself to be part of Christ's continuing incarnation in the flesh and blood of Christ's disciples. Christians need to understand themselves to be Christ's continuing incarnation in the world as Christ's ambassadors

Feel called? Feel compelled by the love of Jesus to cross some thresholds? Do you have the sense that you simply must do this thing, engage this particular group of people, respond to this particular need in the community? Don't talk yourself out of it! The answer to "How" is "Yes." Practice "The Gospel according to Nike" and "just do it." Move. Start. Others will join you.

- **OPEN YOUR EYES:** What needs do you see around? What makes you righteously angry or hooks your compassion?

- **DESCRIBE YOUR MINISTRY:** How would you describe your ministry at home, at work, in your neighborhood and community, in and through the church?

- **DISCERN "WIJD":** What is Jesus doing in your community? According to his patterns and habits recorded in the Gospels, with whom is he hanging out, standing up for, befriending and healing? How can you join him there?

- **NAME YOUR FEARS:** What thresholds and fears are keeping you from activating and engaging your gifts and sense of calling into the ministry of Jesus?

- **MENTOR:** To whom might you pass the mantle of ministry? With whom might you partner as co-ministers and co-missioners?

Prayer

Lord Jesus, help me see with your eyes, love with your love, cross the lines of my own fears and the warnings of others, and enlist others in your ministries of healing and wholeness.

———

THE MINISTRY OF ALL CHRISTIANS
Day 20
"The Equipping Ministry Staff"

1 Peter 2:9-10 (NRSV)

[9] But you are a chosen race, a royal priesthood, a holy nation, God's own people, in order that you may proclaim the mighty acts of him who called you out of darkness into his marvelous light. [10] Once you were not a people, but now you are God's people; once you had not received mercy, but now you have received mercy.

> *Greater is the one who multiplies the workers than the one who does the work.*
> John Raleigh Mott

> *It's better to put ten people to work than to do the work of ten people.*
> D.L. Moody

> *The pastor is not the chief equipper of the saints, but rather is one of many who give leadership to the systemic life of the church so that the church as a whole lives consistently and congruently with its true biblical identity: the people of God invested in the world for Christ and his kingdom.*
> The Equipping Pastor

We are in a service economy. We have become used to hiring specialized service providers or professionals to do everything from teaching our children to changing our oil.

We go to specific places and receive the services of designated people in a highly specialized and compartmentalized culture. We pay people to cook our food, entertain us, train us, heal us, and be ministers for us. As we move away from an economy built predominately on manufacturing and toward and economy built on people performing services for other people, churches can drift into a "payment for services rendered" culture. In such a culture we expect to get what we pay for. It's a transaction of money and other compensation for checking off the tasks on a job description.

In the contemporary Church, many people see the ministry staff as service providers: services like planning and delivering worship services, including preaching sermons, providing music, and recruiting and coaching support groups like ushers, acolytes, and the altar guild. We expect to pay a professional to direct a choir or a worship band, manage the property and physical assets, start Sunday school classes and small groups, and provide programs for children, youth, and adults at various stages of life.

Becoming an equipping congregation involves a radical shift away from this kind of service provider model. In the shift from a staff-driven menu of ministry services and programs to a Spirit-led, gifts-based model of every-member-ministry, it's easy to get frustrated. I had one man tell me it was my responsibility as "the minister of this church to get us some new members and raise more money to meet the budget." I've actually had more than one church member ask, "What are we paying *you* for?"

———

But, I am not **the** minister of any church or any church program or ministry. As the Church, we are all ministers. When The Bridge Church in Springhill, Tennessee hired a young man named Craig in the areas of youth ministry and connecting new members into the live and ministry of the church, they tried to help their members understand the role of all ministry staff by being clear about the role of their newest staff member. Here's what they wrote on their website about Craig:

> In light of Ephesians 4:11-13, Craig:
> - **ISN'T** to be The Bridge's Student Minister.
> - **IS** to invest in and raise up ("equip") the people in our church body that God is calling and gifting to be Student Ministers.
> - **ISN'T** to be The Bridge's Children's Minister.
> - **IS** to identify the people in our church body who are uniquely empowered to lead this ministry better than he could and to invest in them and raise them up to be children's ministers.

It's hard for the staff. Some ministry staff have a long history of being a service providers, of being needed. Much of their identity may be wrapped up in doing ministry tasks. I've had more than one ministry staff member, including pastors, ask me, "If I equip others to do ministry, what will my role be?" My only answer is, "Exactly! That IS your role!"

———

It's hard for church members. We've been in a staff-driven, service-providing model for so long, it's hard to imagine another way. It's more efficient. It's more centralized. After all, staff members have special training and experience, and they have time to take care of the details, make the arrangements, and provide the leadership. It's their job.

But it will become even harder if we don't move away from a staff-driven, program oriented ministry to a Spirit-gifted, mission-driven, ministry of the laity.

Our church has moved from listing ministry staff by title toward associating staff with areas of ministry that they help shepherd. Instead of providing ministry services and programs, ministry staff mentor and empower member-ministers into ministry and service based on their gifts and passions for particular ministries.

- **ASK:** Ask yourself, "What is my ministry? To what avenue of service in and through, and even as the church, am I equipped and called?"

- **CHANGE:** Ask yourself, "In what specific ways do I need to change the way I think about 'ministry' and those our congregation pays as ministry staff?"

- **NAME YOUR FEARS:** What is scary about moving away from a model that pays for ministry services and moves toward a model that pays for guidance and mentorship for equipping and releasing member-ministers for doing their ministries?

- **CONFIDE:** Go to your pastor or other members of your congregation's ministry staff and have a frank conversation, maybe even a time of confession and repentance on both sides, about your long-held assumptions and expectations of those designated and paid for ministry.

Prayer

Meditate on Matthew 18:18, "Whatever you bind on earth will be bound in heaven, and whatever you loose on earth will be loosed in heaven." Then pray this breath prayer:

Lord Jesus, help me do my part to release my sisters and brothers in Christ from the prison of my expectations. Amen.

The Gifted Church

THE MINISTRY OF ALL CHRISTIANS
Day 21
"There's Something You Should Know"

1 Corinthians 12:1-3 (MSG)
[1] What I want to talk about now is the various ways God's Spirit gets worked into our lives. This is complex and often misunderstood, but I want you to be informed and knowledgeable. [2] Remember how you were when you didn't know God, led from one phony god to another, never knowing what you were doing, just doing it because everybody else did it? It's different in this life. God wants us to use our intelligence, to seek to understand as well as we can. [3] For instance, by using your heads, you know perfectly well that the Spirit of God would never prompt anyone to say "Jesus be damned!" Nor would anyone be inclined to say, "Jesus is Master!" without the insight of the Holy Spirit.

> *Education is learning what you didn't even know you didn't know.*
>   Daniel J. Boorstin

> *Being ignorant is not so much a shame as being unwilling to learn.*
>   Benjamin Franklin

> **Dorothy:** *Will you help me? Can you help me?*
> **Glinda:** *You don't need to be helped any longer. You've always had the power to go back to Kansas.*
> **Dorothy:** *I have?*
> **Scarecrow:** *Then why didn't you tell her before?*

———

> **Glinda:** *Because she wouldn't have believed me. She had to learn it for herself.*
> Scene from *The Wiazrd of Oz*

Ignorance may be bliss, but it can be devastating as well. Not to know about a life-threatening disease may allow someone to go through life with a naïve happiness, but without the treatment that could have cured the condition. On the other hand, one might struggle along in life, unaware of a wealth of resources they could have had at their disposal had they known. Either way, ignorance is a problem.

For many years a certain man dreamed of taking a cruise. He looked through travel folders and studied the glossy photos of deep blue water and white sand. He worked hard and finally saved enough money to purchase a ticket on a beautiful ship bound for a week in the Caribbean. But he didn't quite understand the process. He thought he could not possibly afford both to make the voyage and to eat in the expensive looking restaurants in the colorful brochure he'd received from the cruise line, so he brought his own food with him – a week's supply of peanut butter and crackers. For the first several days that's all he ate for breakfast, lunch, and dinner.

Finally, he noticed everyone else gathering around the fancy tables enjoying steak and lobster, or walking through the long buffet lines loaded with everything imaginable.

———

He approached one of the stewards and said desperately, "I'll do anything to get just one meal. Put me to work. I'll earn it." The steward was puzzled by the request. He said, "But you bought passage on this cruise." "Yes," the passenger answered. "Well, didn't you understand that the meals were included in the price? You can eat all you want anytime you want."

I can't imagine anyone actually booking a cruise without that piece of knowledge (in fact, that is one of the reasons some of us would want to sail in the first place), but that is just the way Christian people often live out life in Christ. Out of ignorance of what God has done for them in Christ they survive on a peanut-butter-and-crackers kind of experience.

Paul affirms to the Corinthians that he desires for them to be well informed about "spiritual gifts" (1 Cor. 12:1). Ignorance about the reality and existence of spiritual gifts leaves some Christians believing and behaving as if they have nothing to offer the mission of God in their church. They see others as the gifted ones. Ignorance about the nature of the gifts leaves some followers of Jesus struggling hard to do things they are not equipped to do rather than finding the joy of engaging the calling that is theirs. Ignorance about the working of the various gifts sometimes produces conflict among believers who act out of pride or selfishness. Ignorance about the importance of spiritual gifts can leave the local church crippled as it attempts to carry out its mission with only a portion of its body parts functioning.

———

When we confess that Jesus is Lord, becoming one of his followers, we were at that moment gifted with the presence of God's Holy Spirit in our lives. That includes the unique gifting that is ours to contribute to the life and mission of God's Church.

- **KNOW THYSELF:** What gift is yours? In what ways do you believe that God has gifted you to serve his church and his world?

- **KNOW HOW YOU ARE KNOWN BY OTHERS:** How would others who know you well describe your giftedness?

- **LET NEEDS YOU NOTICE CALL FORTH YOUR GIFTS:** Sometimes our giftedness may be discerned by observing the things in the church and the world that need attention. What needs in the life of the church or people in your world do you tend to notice most?

Prayer
Lord Jesus, teach us to understand the gifts that are ours and the ways in which you want to use us in your mission.

THE MINISTRY OF ALL CHRISTIANS
Day 22
"Recognize the Gift Giver"

1 Corinthians 12:4-7 (NKJV)
[4] There are diversities of gifts, but the same Spirit. [5] There are differences of ministries, but the same Lord. [6] And there are diversities of activities, but it is the same God who works all in all. [7] But the manifestation of the Spirit is given to each one for the profit *of all.*

> *He who loves with purity considers not the gift of the lover, but the love of the giver.*
> Thomas Kempis

> *When you have been given something in a moment of grace, it is sacrilegious to be greedy.*
> Marian Anderson

> *What we are is God's gift to us. What we become is our gift to God.*
> Eleanor Powell

How disappointing it would be as a parent to carefully select a gift for your child as an expression of your love, only to have that child refuse to open it. Or how frustrating it would be to have your spouse take a look at a gift you'd thoughtfully picked out for a special occasion, and then close the box and set it aside.

Perhaps it would be even more discouraging for someone you love deeply to receive the gift only to become so enamored with the gift that they ceased caring for you!

Paul goes to some lengths to affirm that spiritual gifts have been given to us by the Father, Son, and Spirit. God himself is the source of these capacities we have for service in the Body of Christ. The gifts may vary among us, but they have all been given by the same Spirit. We may employ these gifts in a multitude of different settings, but they are all offered as service to the same Lord Jesus. Some may be far more proficient in the exercise of their gifts than others, but all receive their power for ministry from the same God. God is the Gift Giver.

Since these gifts have come to our lives from God himself, we cannot refuse to receive them. Nor can we refuse to use them. Nor should we become so wrapped up in our own gift that we forget the Giver himself. Consider the appropriate response to a gift offered by someone who loves you and who has thoughtfully and generously selected something for you. You joyfully receive it. You admire the package. You read the card. You say "thank you." And then you open it, admire it, and say thanks a few more times.

You make the gift a part of your life. You wear the sweater. You put on the jewelry. You try out the power tool. You show it off and say thanks again. You may set it down and walk over to the giver and offer an expression of your affection and gratitude.

———

In the case of spiritual gifts, an appropriate response is much the same. Joyfully receive the fact that you are indeed gifted by God for his service. Learn to discover and identify your particular gift. Esteem and value it and note its value to the Body of Christ. Learn what you can about how to use that gift. Find others who share it and learn from them. Say thank you to God. Make the gift a part of your life. Make your life a gift. Begin to use it in service, and say thanks a few more times.

- **GIVE THANKS:** What is one way you can best express your gratitude to God for the gifts you have received? A prayer? A journal entry? A testimony to a friend?

- **IMPROVE:** How can you develop the gift or gifts you have received so that they might be used even more effectively in service? What would be a next step?

Prayer
Lord Jesus, thank you so much for extending your grace in the form of the gifts you have given for me to use in your service.

NOTES:

THE MINISTRY OF ALL CHRISTIANS
Day 23
"They Are All So Different"

1 Corinthians 12:7-11 (NRSV)

[7] To each is given the manifestation of the Spirit for the common good. [8] To one is given through the Spirit the utterance of wisdom, and to another the utterance of knowledge according to the same Spirit, [9] to another faith by the same Spirit, to another gifts of healing by the one Spirit, [10] to another the working of miracles, to another prophecy, to another the discernment of spirits, to another various kinds of tongues, to another the interpretation of tongues. [11] All these are activated by one and the same Spirit, who allots to each one individually just as the Spirit chooses.

Variety is the spice of life.
American proverb

Diversity is not about how we differ. Diversity is about embracing one another's uniqueness.
Ola Joseph

Infinite diversity in infinite combinations... symbolizing the elements that create truth and beauty.
Commander Spock

It is time for parents to teach young people early on that in diversity there is beauty and there is strength.
Maya Angelou

"I don't know how those two boys could be related," Carol sighed. She was talking about her own sons. Matt, the eldest, was outgoing, athletic, and somewhat demanding. Kent, the younger, was reserved, musical, and seemed to take things in stride. Both had the same parents and were raised in the same home. But they were so different!

The same question can be raised in our churches. One Christian leader in the congregation sees the tasks that need to be done, thinks in terms of how to strategize and organize in order to accomplish them, and has the ability to motivate others to join her. Another is sensitive to the needs of hurting people and moves quietly and responsively to their side. Yet another finds in the study and teaching of Scripture enough to occupy his attention and energy week after week. How can followers of Jesus be so differently motivated? They have been redeemed by the same Savior. They serve the same Lord. They are filled with the same Spirit, yet they are so different!

The fact is, we are supposed to be different. We are distinct from each other as the parts of our body are different. A hand is not a foot. A foot is not an ear. Our fingers are not our heart. Although they were generated in the same embryonic process in the womb as we were formed, they are so different, however, it is their distinctiveness that makes each one necessary and useful. All the tasks of living are addressed because our bodies have such a variety of parts.

Here's what the differences mean, according to Paul. It means that none of us is left out. It means that we don't have to be like everyone else.

The "manifestation of the Spirit for the common good" is given to each of us (v. 7). The gift God has given me is what God expects me to use. The gift God has given you is the one God expects you to use. We do not have to be just alike. I'm free not to be jealous of your gift and not to impose mine upon you.

Are you clear about the gifts that the Spirit has given to you? They are meant to be used in service to Christ and his Church. Do you see the gifts that have been given to others in the congregation? Those are to be celebrated as well. The Good News is that God incorporates each of us into the Church by means of gifts given for the common good. Those gifts, like the different parts of our body, complement each other and serve each other.

What a wonderful thing it is that we are not all alike! Some of us would then be unnecessary, and we would not, in fact, be a body at all, let alone The Body of Christ!

- **THINK** carefully about the things that make you distinct from others.
    - What gifts do you have?
    - What is your passion or heart for ministry?
    - What abilities have you acquired over the years?
    - What characterizes your personality?
    - What experiences have you had in life and ministry?
    - List those unique aspects of who you are and celebrate them in prayer.

____

- **CONSIDER** the person in your circle of friends or family who is the most different from you.
  - What are the unique qualities they bring to your church and its life?
  - List them and celebrate those in prayer as well.

Prayer
Lord, help me today to see and to celebrate the different gifts you have given to my brothers and sisters in our church family.

———

THE MINISTRY OF ALL CHRISTIANS
Day 24
"We Are All One"

1 Corinthians 12:12-20 (The Message)
[12] You can easily enough see how this kind of thing works by looking no further than your own body. Your body has many parts—limbs, organs, cells—but no matter how many parts you can name, you're still one body. It's exactly the same with Christ. [13] By means of his one Spirit, we all said good-bye to our partial and piecemeal lives. We each used to independently call our own shots, but then we entered into a large and integrated life in which he has the final say in everything. (This is what we proclaimed in word and action when we were baptized.) Each of us is now a part of his resurrection body, refreshed and sustained at one fountain—his Spirit—where we all come to drink. The old labels we once used to identify ourselves—labels like Jew or Greek, slave or free—are no longer useful. We need something larger, more comprehensive. [14] I want you to think about how all this makes you more significant, not less. A body isn't just a single part blown up into something huge. It's all the different-but-similar parts arranged and functioning together. [15] If Foot said, "I'm not elegant like Hand, embellished with rings; I guess I don't belong to this body," would that make it so? [16] If Ear said, "I'm not beautiful like Eye, limpid and expressive; I don't deserve a place on the head," would you want to remove it from the body? [17] If the body was all eye, how could it hear? If all ear, how could it smell? [18]

As it is, we see that God has carefully placed each part of the body right where he wanted it. [19] But I also want you to think about how this keeps your significance from getting blown up into self-importance. For no matter how significant you are, it is only because of what you are a part of. An enormous eye or a gigantic hand wouldn't be a body, but a monster. [20] What we have is one body with many parts, each its proper size and in its proper place. No part is important on its own.

Has it ever occurred to you that one hundred pianos all tuned to the same fork are automatically tuned to each other? They are of one accord by being tuned, not to each other, but to another standard to which each one must individually bow. So one hundred worshippers meeting together, each one looking away to Christ, are in heart nearer to each other than they could possibly be were they to become "unity" conscious and turn their eyes away from God to strive for closer fellowship. Social religion is perfected when private religion is purified.
A.W. Tozer

Diversity is the magic. It is the first manifestation, the first beginning of the differentiation of a thing and of simple identity. The greater the diversity, the greater the perfection.
Thomas Berry

———

The United States of America was once described as a "melting pot," where immigrants from many parts of the world, representing a smorgasbord of cultures, a plethora of traditions, and a variety of religious backgrounds had come together as "Americans." The trouble is, the melting did not always happen. People came with their unique foods, holidays, languages, and folkways and often held on to those distinctive cultural features. They became Americans, all right, part of the "one nation under God," but they just never completely melted.

That reality has been bothersome to some, who would like each and every one to be just like themselves. However, most see that diversity as a strength to our culture. Who wants to live in a place that doesn't offer enchiladas, lasagna, AND sweet and sour chicken? The various ethnic folk festivals celebrated around our land provide color and texture to the landscape. True, those differences sometimes present a challenge. Yet the benefit has proven to be worth the effort.

The Church is not a melting pot, either. We bring our unique and distinct gifts to the body of Christ. We do not expect each one to be just like the other. Paul exaggerates the issue to the point of ridicule: "What if the whole body were just an eye? How would we hear anything?" The mental image of the body as a giant ear or foot reveals just how ridiculous it is for someone to insist on uniformity or to move toward division over differences rather than to work for unity among the diversity.

———

We need to be different from one another in order to be the Body. One of us, or a bunch of us who are all the same, cannot express the fullness of Christ's ministry in this world. We need to be different.

Yet we need to be one. Our unity cannot be found in uniformity, however. It is found in our mutual service to each other, our common submission to Christ as Lord, our universal experience of the Spirit of God in our lives, and our belonging to one body. We can never insist that others be just like us in their gifts and service. Nor can we envy the gifts that they have. We all bring our gifts to serve Christ together, and together we are able to be the Body of Christ in the world, continuing his messianic mission of declaring the reality of the Kingdom of God. Rather than melting into a single substance, we join together with a single heart and purpose.

- **TRY TO SEE IT THROUGH GOD'S EYES:** How would you describe the purpose of the Church? What is it that God is up to in the world through the Church?

- **TRANSLATE THAT INTO YOUR TIME AND PLACE:** How would you describe the purpose of your own congregation? What distinctive mission or purpose do you share with your fellow Christians at this time and in this place?

- **NOW YOU:** How does who you are (your gifts, heart, abilities, personality, and experience) contribute to those purposes? Why is it important that you identify and claim those distinctive aspects of your life if the Church is to accomplish its purpose?

Prayer

God, help us to find the unity in the Body of Christ you intend your people to know and experience.

NOTES:

THE MINISTRY OF ALL CHRISTIANS
Day 25
"We Are All Dependent"

1 Corinthians 12:21-26 (NRSV)

[21] The eye cannot say to the hand, "I have no need of you," nor again the head to the feet, "I have no need of you." [22] On the contrary, the members of the body that seem to be weaker are indispensable, [23] and those members of the body that we think less honorable we clothe with greater honor, and our less respectable members are treated with greater respect; [24] whereas our more respectable members do not need this. But God has so arranged the body, giving the greater honor to the inferior member, [25] that there may be no dissension within the body, but the members may have the same care for one another. [26] If one member suffers, all suffer together with it; if one member is honored, all rejoice together with it.

Alone we can do so little; together we can do so much.
Helen Keller

Teamwork is the ability to work together toward a common vision. The ability to direct individual accomplishments toward organizational objectives. It is the fuel that allows common people to attain uncommon results.
Andrew Carnegie

Individuals play the game, but teams beat the odds.
A Navy SEAL Team saying

———

The way a team plays as a whole determines its success. You may have the greatest bunch of individual stars in the world, but if they don't play together, the club won't be worth a dime.

Babe Ruth

When it comes to Olympic competition, Jenny Thompson is among the most-decorated athlete in history. Her 12 medals in the 1992, 1996, 2000, and 2004 Olympic Games make her the most decorated woman swimmer ever in any nation. Eight of Jenny Thompson's medals were gold. The irony is that eight of her dozen medals, the gold ones, were won in team competition. She has not won a single individual gold medal at all. Always with a team.

Some have questioned whether Jenny belongs in the list of the great competitors in Olympic sports history because she has never won one by herself. Always with a team. Jenny herself recognized, in an interview after the 2000 Olympics, that winning an individual medal would be a very different experience. When she received her tenth medal, Jenny passed up Bonnie Blair, the skater, as the most decorated American woman Olympic athlete. Bonnie Blair commented, "I wish she could feel what it's like to win an individual gold, to witness it by herself and not as part of a team."

Actually, there's something very attractive about Jenny's accomplishment -- she has repeatedly achieved her victories as part of a successful team.

Many professional athletes today have very little team commitment. They will move from one team to another as best benefits them financially. Team commitment isn't a common value of sports culture. But Jenny has succeeded as part of a team.

Jenny's experience is a model of what it is supposed to be like to be part of the Church. The Church was designed by God from the very beginning to be something that functions as a team, as a body, in which everybody has a part to contribute. When we win, we as a team and when we lose, we lose as a team. There are no individual gold medals in the Kingdom of God. The gold comes to the Church of Jesus Christ. We are learning to be Christ's Body, to work and serve and accomplish his mission as a team. God makes that happen by giving to all the people of the Church the capacities known as spiritual gifts.

These gifts are all vital to our success as God's people. Some gifts may be more prominent than others, but all are necessary. None are to be despised in ourselves or in others, for they have been given by God's Holy Spirit. No one is left out. No one is unimportant. When the team is missing an active member, it suffers in its ability to achieve. So, too, the Church suffers when the gift of any believer is withheld from service.

Be encouraged to know your giftedness, to value the gifts God has give you and others, and to faithfully engage your gift in the life and work of God's people.

- **SEE THE NEEDS:** What are some of the things that need to be done in the life of your church that you are not equipped to do? What are the places in your church that must be filled by others? Can you list five of them? Ten?

- **APPLY YOUR LEARNING:** What does that list say to you about your dependence on others in the church? What does it say about the need of the congregation to function like a team?

Prayer

Lord Jesus, thank you for the gifts you have given your church, for the Spirit who empowers them, and for the glory they bring to the Father as they are offered in service.

THE MINISTRY OF ALL CHRISTIANS
Day 26
"Be the Body"

1 Corinthians 12:27-31 (NRSV)
[27]Now you are the body of Christ and individually members of it. [28]And God has appointed in the church first apostles, second prophets, third teachers; then deeds of power, then gifts of healing, forms of assistance, forms of leadership, various kinds of tongues. [29]Are all apostles? Are all prophets? Are all teachers? Do all work miracles? [30]Do all possess gifts of healing? Do all speak in tongues? Do all interpret? [31]But strive for the greater gifts. And I will show you a still more excellent way.

> *Strange, isn't it? Each man's life touches so many other lives. When he isn't around he leaves an awful hole, doesn't he?*
> Clarence, George Bailey's angel in
> *It's a Wonderful Life*

> *You cannot continuously improve interdependent systems and processes until you progressively perfect interdependent, interpersonal relationships.*
> Stephen Covey

> *But the way people commonly use the word "interdependence" nowadays it means something all of whose parts are mutually interdependent - not only for their mutual action, but for their meaning and for their existence.*
> David Bohm

———

Let's face it. In most of life we really are interdependent. We need each other. Staunch independence is an illusion, but heavy dependence isn't healthy, either. The only position of long-term strength is interdependence: win/win.
Greg Anderson

To observe the human body at work is to witness a miraculous moment that we constantly take for granted. The coordinated work of the many systems -- central nervous, respiratory, digestive, muscular, skeletal, reproductive – allow the human being to think, interact with the world through five senses, move, and create. The skilled actions of an accomplished gymnast in a floor exercise or the quick movements of the fingers of a concert pianist leave us in awe. The body at work is a beautiful and marvelous work of creation.

Paul's metaphor of the Church, and individual churches, as a body is meant to be organic. He wants us to recognize how all the parts work together, how each is necessary, how none are to be despised. We get that, but it struck us as a mysterious and audacious claim that this body of which we are part is none other than Christ's body: "Now you are Christ's body, and individually members of it" (v. 27). It is not simply that we are part of an organic group to which each person contributes functions and service. We are part of Christ's body. Christ's body, not Jesus' body. We are the Body of the Christ, the Body of the Messiah.

———

We, the Church, are the messianic people of God. The Messiah has appeared in human history and we, his followers, take up his mission, each contributing our gifts and abilities humbly and obediently. All are necessary for none of us individually is the Messiah. The Spirit works through God's people to continue the work Jesus the Messiah began. Jesus promised we would do the works he did and even greater ones (John 14:12-13). Acts begins by reminding Theophilus of the stories in the gospel of Luke of all that "Jesus began to do and teach" (Acts 1:1), implying perhaps that this volume will be reporting what the Messiah continues to do and teach through his body, the Church. Perhaps when we live in community and love, share our gifts, and engage his mission, we participate in the Kingdom of God in ways we have not recognized.

Some of us need to be apostles, missionaries taking the gospel of Jesus into those places in our world that are darkest and most in need of light. Some of us need to be prophets, speaking forth the Word of God to the Church and to the world as well. Some need to be teachers who build up the Body of Christ by applying the gospel to their lived lives. Others become instruments of God's power and healing, and others offer helpful guidance and leadership to the Church. All of us together, contributing these Spirit-given gifts, allow the church to be the body of the Messiah in the world and allow the world an opportunity to meet Jesus.

- **THINK AGAIN** about the unique way that God has shaped your life for service: your gifts, passions, abilities, personality, and experiences. Imagine what it would be like for your church to have to do its work without those gifts being offered in service. What will it miss? What will it be unable to do? What needs would go unmet? Can you list three things? Five?

- **IMAGINE** depriving yourself of some part of your physical body. Think of walking through the house with your eyes closed or having to go through the day with your hands tied behind your back. It is not difficult to grasp how important it is for every part of the body to function fully. Offer a prayer or write a covenant in your journal in which you make all that you are available to God through his body the Church.

Prayer
Loving God, help me today to do my part as a member of your body so that together with my brothers and sisters we may powerfully and effectively bear witness to your goodness and grace.

THE MINISTRY OF ALL CHRISTIANS
Day 27
"It's Not the Gift that Matters"

1 Corinthians 13:1-13 (NRSV)

[1] If I speak in the tongues of mortals and of angels, but do not have love, I am a noisy gong or a clanging cymbal. [2] And if I have prophetic powers, and understand all mysteries and all knowledge, and if I have all faith, so as to remove mountains, but do not have love, I am nothing. [3] I f I give away all my possessions, and if I hand over my body so that I may boast, but do not have love, I gain nothing. [4] Love is patient; love is kind; love is not envious or boastful or arrogant [5] or rude. It does not insist on its own way; it is not irritable or resentful; [6] it does not rejoice in wrongdoing, but rejoices in the truth. [7] It bears all things, believes all things, hopes all things, endures all things. [8] Love never ends. But as for prophecies, they will come to an end; as for tongues, they will cease; as for knowledge, it will come to an end. [9] For we know only in part, and we prophesy only in part; [10] but when the complete comes, the partial will come to an end. [11] When I was a child, I spoke like a child, I thought like a child, I reasoned like a child; when I became an adult, I put an end to childish ways. [12] For now we see in a mirror, dimly, but then we will see face to face. Now I know only in part; then I will know fully, even as I have been fully known. [13] And now faith, hope, and love abide, these three; and the greatest of these is love.

Love is the answer to everything. It's the only reason to do anything.
Ray Bradbury

———

Kiss today goodbye, and point me toward tomorrow. We did what we had to do. Won't forget, can't regret what I did for love.
> From "What I Did for Love"
> *A Chorus Line*

Light of the world, shine on me. Love is the answer. Shine on us all, set us free. Love is the answer
> England Dan & John Ford Coley

All you need is love, love, love is all you need.
> Lennon/McCartney

Apparently, early on churches found it a relational challenge to work together as the Body of Christ. So many sinful, selfish inclinations work against such a thing. We may take pride in the gifts we have been given, thinking ourselves better or more important than others. Alternatively, we may despise our gifts and wish we were gifted like someone else in the body. It is not an accident that each time Paul writes about the employment of spiritual gifts, he also writes about unity, humility, and love (see Romans 12 and Ephesians 4 as other examples). Here in the letter to the Corinthians, he devotes three chapters to the subject of spiritual giftedness. In the very heart of that discussion he nestles 1 Corinthians 13, the well-known "Love Chapter."

Although these words of Paul, beautiful and poetic, are often lifted out of this context and read on their own, the context really matters.

The call to sacrificial Christian love sounds amid the struggle of God's people to exercise their gifts and to be the Body of Christ. Love is the lubricant that reduces friction and allows people to work together in unity.

Jesus made it clear that the call on our lives is essentially relational. No greater commandments exist than these two: Love God wholeheartedly and love your neighbor unselfishly. This is the very essence of human life as God intended it. It is life redeemed and restored in Christ. It really is that simple. We are called to love God and to love people.

The 13th chapter of 1 Corinthians, often quoted, frequently framed, widely known, is seldom lived. These words describe behavior, not feeling. In the Western world, love is understood as a feeling state. In this passage, love is a condition of the will. One loves not because of a feeling, but because of a great commandment. The condition of the beloved is not at issue here either. We are not called to be patient or kind with people because of who they are, but because of who we are. Is there a clearer description of spiritual maturity anywhere in Scripture?

These few sentences describe so well the life of Jesus. Love is a choice to act on behalf of the good of another person. So kindness, patience, gentleness, and all the qualities of love are the fruit of the redeemed will. Being the Body of Christ means living together as Jesus lived his own life – out of sacrificial love.

Here is the call of God to us: Pursue love! Love wholeheartedly! Love unselfishly! We hear the command and we hesitate. How presumptuous of us to think that we could love like Jesus! We protest our inadequacy before the fiery bush summoning us to a new life. God's response is the same to us: "I will be with you. I who am love will teach you how to love. Follow me. It is not up to you. Go and love whomever I send you to. I will be with you." Once more the best response is not presumption or reluctance, but obedient faith.

- **READ:** Read through 1 Corinthians 13:4-7, the characteristic behaviors of love, and substitute the word "Jesus" for love. Does the passage still make sense? Now substitute your own name. Which of those characteristics do you believe most needs to be developed in your own life and character? How would your life be different if you were to grow in love in that way?

- **PRAY or WRITE:** Spiritual formation is about becoming like Christ, being formed into Christ's image. Offer a prayer or write one in your journal, asking God to form one particular aspect of love more fully in your life.

Prayer
God of love, we know so little about that word we use so often, so we must depend on you to teach us and to give us power through your Spirit to love as you command.

———

NOTES:

The Missional Church

THE MINISTRY OF ALL CHRISTIANS
Day 28
"Thank God for a Church on Mission"

Romans 1:8-13 (NRSV)

[8] First, I thank my God through Jesus Christ for all of you, because your faith is proclaimed throughout the world. [9] For God, whom I serve with my spirit by announcing the gospel of his Son, is my witness that without ceasing I remember you always in my prayers, [10] asking that by God's will I may somehow at last succeed in coming to you. [11] For I am longing to see you so that I may share with you some spiritual gift to strengthen you— [12] or rather so that we may be mutually encouraged by each other's faith, both yours and mine. [13] I want you to know, brothers and sisters, that I have often intended to come to you (but thus far have been prevented), in order that I may reap some harvest among you as I have among the rest of the Gentiles.

> *The question is not whether or not the church has a mission. The question is will God's mission have a church? If there be no mission there can be no discipleship, and if there is no discipleship there will be no mission.*
> Alan Hirsch

> *The mark of a great church is not its seating capacity, but its sending capacity.*
> Mike Stachura

———

What a relief it is to realize that the mission of the Church is actually the mission of God! Our task is to grasp what God has been doing redemptively in the world and to engage that mission. We are not charged with inventing a mission, but are invited to join one that has been in progress for thousands of years.

God is at work gathering a people from every tongue and language and nation who love God wholeheartedly and who love each other unselfishly. Beginning at least with the call of Abraham (Gen. 12:1-3), extending to the covenant with Israel at Mt. Sinai (Ex. 19-20), and continuing through the period of the judges and the kings, God has been at work. Refining the people of God through the Exile and graciously restoring them to the land, God has been on mission.

Preserving Israel through the oppression of the Greeks and Romans, God has been at work. Preparing the world for the coming of Christ, God has been on mission (Gal. 4:4). When Jesus gathered disciples and instructed them, God was on mission. On the cross and at the empty tomb, God's mission continued. On the day of Pentecost, pouring out the Holy Spirit on the Church, God powerfully advanced that mission (Acts 1-2). As the Church took the good news of Jesus to the ends of the earth, God's mission unfolded (Acts 8-28). Down through history for the past two thousand years, God's mission has moved forward. We who now are followers of Jesus step into something that long preceded us and that is so much bigger than we are!

———

As Paul opens the epistle to the Romans, that great exposition on the mission of God in Christ, he does so with an expression of gratitude. Paul is thankful for the ways in which the Roman church has already been participating in the mission of God. He is grateful for their faith in Christ, which has begun to spread throughout the world.

One of the richest experiences of life is being part of a church whose heart is for the mission of God. Such a church is regularly, prayerfully asking the question "Where is God at work in our world? Where can we join God in that work?" Such a missional church is generous, selfless, and alive. Such a church asks its members to discover the gifts the Spirit has given them and challenges them to engage those gifts in service. Congregations like that understand that they are in fact the Body of Christ, the Body of the Messiah, extending the messianic mission into the world as the Spirit of God empowers them.

If you know the privilege of being part of such a church, give thanks to God for that wonderful gift.

- **RECALL:** What is one specific way you have seen your own church respond to the mission of God in the world? How did you participate in that response?

- **PAY ATTENTION:** Where are you sensing God to be at work in your world in such a way that you or your congregation may be receiving a divine invitation to participate?

———

- **PRAY:** Spend some time praying for a clear sense of calling and direction about adjusting your life and moving forward in obedience to God's invitation to join the mission.

Prayer

Lord God, who in pursuit of the mission of reconciling the world to yourself did not spare even your own Son, but freely delivered him up for us, help us by your power to freely give ourselves to the work and message of the good news.

———

THE MINISTRY OF ALL CHRISTIANS
Day 29
"Thank God for a Gifted Church"

1 Corinthians 1:4-9 (NRSV)
[4] I give thanks to my God always for you because of the grace of God that has been given you in Christ Jesus, [5] for in every way you have been enriched in him, in speech and knowledge of every kind— [6] just as the testimony of Christ has been strengthened among you— [7] so that you are not lacking in any spiritual gift as you wait for the revealing of our Lord Jesus Christ. [8] He will also strengthen you to the end, so that you may be blameless on the day of our Lord Jesus Christ. [9] God is faithful; by him you were called into the fellowship of his Son, Jesus Christ our Lord.

> *Coming together is a beginning; keeping together is progress; working together is success.*
> Henry Ford

> *A dream you dream alone is only a dream. A dream you dream together is reality.*
> Yoko Ono

> *Home wasn't a set house, or a single town on a map. It was wherever the people who loved you were, whenever you were together. Not a place, but a moment, and then another, building on each other like bricks to create a solid shelter that you take with you for your entire life, wherever you may go.*
> Sarah Dessen,
> *What Happened to Goodbye*

I served for 22 years as the pastor of a congregation of richly gifted people. They were bright, well educated, highly trained, influential in the world, and fairly affluent. They could do almost anything they wanted to in their lives, but they possessed yet another resource that could not be earned, purchased, or acquired by any human effort: they were people gifted by the Holy Spirit to do the work of Christ in the world.

Some among us were prophets. They saw what was right and wrong in the world and spoke that to our congregation and its leaders. Some were teachers. They valued the truth, loved to study Scripture, and were skilled in sharing their knowledge with others. Some were evangelists whose hearts were tender toward those who did not yet know Christ and who helped others learn to share their faith. Some had gifts of mercy and expressed Christ's compassion toward the hurting. Some had gifts of administration and helped us organize to do God's work. Some had gifts of faith, some gifts of help, and others gifts of generosity. I'm not even certain I could enumerate all the ways in which the Spirit graciously gave to us the abilities we needed to do the work we were called to do together, however, it was clear that there were gifts planted throughout the congregation that made it possible for us to do together things none of us could ever do on our own.

Those gifts were paired with hearts of passion about certain issues or particular human hurts and hopes. Some had a heart for teenagers, some for children, and some for adults at various stages of life.

———

These ministers of the Gospel took their gifts of teaching, mercy, and administration and brought them to bear on those lives. Some had a heart for the poor, those struggling with domestic violence, or those seeking recovery from addictions. They exercised their giftedness in that context. Some focused on the needs of the Navaho Nation in Arizona and New Mexico. Some attended to the health care needs of the poor in Oaxaca, Mexico. Some took their giftedness to a local apartment ministry or into a partnership with a nearby elementary school. Their hearts and their gifts allowed the ministry of Christ to become real in the lives of people.

I witnessed the way those gifts and passions combined with other factors in the lives of God's people. People differed in personality styles: some were more people-focused and some more task-focused; some were more introverted and some more extroverted. Those four factors combined with each other in a variety of ways, and those combinations mixed with various gifts and passions. Additionally, people brought a variety of acquired abilities with them to the tasks, and they brought a wide spectrum of life experiences. All these elements interacted so that this gifted body of people, with many experiences and abilities, varied personalities, and deep but different passions, found innumerable ways of responding to the call of God.

That's the story of any church whose members see themselves as the Body of Christ, respond to God's call to his mission, identify and develop their giftedness, and learn to respond in obedience.

———

To be part of a church learning to live in such a way is to resonate with Paul's expression of gratitude for the Corinthian church, troubled as it was in so many ways: "[4] I give thanks to my God always for you because of the grace of God that has been given you in Christ Jesus, [5] for in every way you have been enriched in him, in speech and knowledge of every kind— [6] just as the testimony of Christ has been strengthened among you— [7] so that you are not lacking in any spiritual gift as you wait for the revealing of our Lord Jesus Christ." (1 Cor. 1:4-7)

- **LIST** as many gifted people in your congregation as you can in three minutes. What are their names? What are their gifts? How have you seen them at work?

- **SPEND A FEW MINUTES** giving thanks to God for each of these fellow disciples and their gifts, expressing your gratitude for what God has done in and through their lives. Why not send a "thank you" email to a few of them with a specific word of encouragement about their gift and their faithfulness?

Prayer
Thank you, Lord God, for the privilege of being part of your people, recipients of all necessary gifts to carry out a mission that infused our lives with meaning and brings the good news of Christ's salvation to the world.

THE MINISTRY OF ALL CHRISTIANS
Day 30
"Thank God for a Missional Partnership"

Philippians 1:3-11 (NRSV)

[3] I thank my God every time I remember you, [4] constantly praying with joy in every one of my prayers for all of you, [5] because of your sharing in the gospel from the first day until now. [6] I am confident of this, that the one who began a good work among you will bring it to completion by the day of Jesus Christ. [7] It is right for me to think this way about all of you, because you hold me in your heart, for all of you share in God's grace with me, both in my imprisonment and in the defense and confirmation of the gospel. [8] For God is my witness, how I long for all of you with the compassion of Christ Jesus. [9] And this is my prayer, that your love may overflow more and more with knowledge and full insight [10] to help you to determine what is best, so that in the day of Christ you may be pure and blameless, [11] having produced the harvest of righteousness that comes through Jesus Christ for the glory and praise of God.

> *For pastors to burn without being consumed*
> *we need companionship for the journey,*
> *people who continue to stoke our faith with*
> *ever more challenging fuel.*
> > Kenda Creasy Dean & Ron Foster,
> > *The Godbearing Life*

> *Called as partners in Christ's service,*
> *Called to ministries of grace,*
> *We respond with deep commitment*
> *Fresh new lines of faith to trace.*

———

May we learn the art of sharing,
Side by side and friend with friend,
Equal partners in our caring
To fulfill God's chosen end.

> Jane Parker Huber, "Called as Partners in Christ's Service"[4]

In his classic little work, *Leadership is an Art,* Max Dupree describes as simply as possible the tasks of "artful leadership": "The first responsibility of a leader is to define reality. The last is to say thank you. In between the two, the leader must become a servant and a debtor. That sums up the progress of an artful leader" (p. 9). The apostle Paul works at that first task through his own preaching and teaching in Philippi as he declares the Kingdom of God (Acts 16). In his absence, his cohorts (Timothy, Silas, and Luke) develop that initial work. His beautiful epistle to his friends further clarifies the reality in which Jesus' followers live and serve.

The second task of the artful leader, becoming a servant and a debtor, Paul accomplishes fully with his churches. He even employs terms like "servant" and "debtor" to describe himself. Sacrificially, he travels, endures persecution and other hardships, prays, and works to be sure his churches could thrive in the hostile pagan environment in which they had been planted.

In the opening words of most of his letters, Paul addresses the third task of artful leadership – gratitude.

---

[4] The Westminster Press (1981)

Paul is grateful both to God and to his friends in the churches, and says so. In particular, his gratitude to God for the people of Philippi literally fills and overflows his heart. He is thankful, he says, for the "partnership in the gospel" (v. 5) he has shared with them from the first day they met until this present moment in which he writes to them from a Roman prison. This "partnership" or "fellowship" is precious to him. Paul uses the Greek word *koinonia* that so beautifully expresses life in the early Christian community. It means a sharing of life at a deep level.

The early church was noted for that experience (Acts 2:42-47) of *koinonia*. It is also used to describe the intimacy between God and the people of God. We have "fellowship" with God and with one another (1 John 1:1-8). The intimate sharing of life that develops between believers who engage the mission of God together is one of the richest experiences of life. The bond that can develop between pastors and churches who work together on the mission, without personal agendas, is among the most precious experiences of the Christian life. For this great gift that Paul and the Philippians have known together, Paul offers his constant gratitude to God.

If you have ever known, as a team leader or team member, the joy of working with brothers and sisters in Christ to engage the mission of God, you have tasted this good gift of God. Serving together on a short-term mission trip, taking on a ministry together weekly, even a single day in service alongside a fellow Christian accomplishes amazing things in our relationships.

———

Spending years or decades serving alongside one another in a congregation, takes that even deeper. If that good gift has been yours, why not pause for a moment and thank God for the "fellowship in the gospel" you have come to know.

- **MAKE A LIST:** Who are your "partners in the gospel"? With whom have you shared experiences of ministry and mission? Make a list.

- **PRAY:** Spend a few minutes in prayer for these, recalling before God the shared times of service that have linked your life with theirs.

- **CONTACT:** Why not send another couple of encouraging, grateful notes out by email today, letting these brothers and sister know how much that shared time has meant to you?

Prayer
Lord God, how can we express the gratitude we feel as we remember those we have been privileged to labor alongside in your Name? You have been gracious to us to allow this in our lives. Thank you for the fellowship in the gospel that has been ours.

THE MINISTRY OF ALL CHRISTIANS
Day 31
"Equipping and External Focus"

Acts 6:1-7 (NRSV)

[1] Now during those days, when the disciples were increasing in number, the Hellenists complained against the Hebrews because their widows were being neglected in the daily distribution of food. [2] And the twelve called together the whole community of the disciples and said, "It is not right that we should neglect the word of God in order to wait on tables. [3] Therefore, friends, select from among yourselves seven men of good standing, full of the Spirit and of wisdom, whom we may appoint to this task, [4] while we, for our part, will devote ourselves to prayer and to serving the word." [5] What they said pleased the whole community, and they chose Stephen, a man full of faith and the Holy Spirit, together with Philip, Prochorus, Nicanor, Timon, Parmenas, and Nicolaus, a proselyte of Antioch. [6] They had these men stand before the apostles, who prayed and laid their hands on them. [7] The word of God continued to spread; the number of the disciples increased greatly in Jerusalem, and a great many of the priests became obedient to the faith.

> *No strategy, tactics, or clever marketing campaign could ever clear away the smokescreen that surrounds Christianity in today's culture. The perception of outsiders will change only when Christians strive to represent the heart of God in every relationship and situation.*
> Kinnaman & Lyons, *Unchristian*

———

...I face a big challenge because every time Christians step inside a church, it can remove them from the very place where they have the greatest impact for God's Kingdom--the world. It's sad, but I wonder if we've inadvertently designed our ministries to isolate Christians from the places where God really wants them to be.

Tony Morgan, *Killing Cockroaches and other Scattered Musings on Leadership*

Most of us spend the majority of our time at home, at work, or at what Ray Oldenburg in *The Great Good Place* calls the "third place." Your "third place" may be Starbucks, Barnes and Noble, the YMCA, on one of the online social networks, in your car shuffling children from one activity to another, or anywhere you may find yourself. Chris is an example of someone who has carried his ministry beyond the walls of his church into his work place. He came up to me after worship one Sunday with a big smile on his face saying, "I realized this week that I am a minister. People come to me at work just to talk because they know I will listen. I recently started a Bible study during lunch and several people attend regularly." Chris practices a ministry of presence and teaching in his workplace. He is a minister as are hundreds of others in our congregations. Stories like Chris's put a smile on my face too! His ministry puts a smile on the faces of many.

At a conference I recently attended, one of the leaders said, "You cannot be an equipping church without being externally focused." Someone else put it this way, "Jesus has left the building." How true and profound these statements are! God's equipped people belong in the world. Ministry practiced only within the walls of a church is nothing more than a Christian club in which Jesus is the mascot. What if we stopped talking about going to "a" church and started thinking of ourselves as "the" Church? What if we began to recognize ourselves as ministers and to acknowledge the many things we already do in ministry? What if we were to find ways to be ministers of the Church all the time in our first, second, and third places? Imagine the impact. We could change the world!

YOU are a Minister
The World needs YOU

- **RECOGNIZE THE NEED:** (Acts 6:1) You are gifted and you are a minister. Have you thought about the fact that you can be a minister in your first, second, and third places?

- **COMMISSION:** (Acts 6:5-6) The Church as incarnated in our churches must be in constant prayer for its gifted and equipped ministers. Does your church pray for all of its ministers on a regular basis? Not only are these prayers for the clergy; they should also be for you. Remember, you are a minister.

- **SEND:** (Acts 6:2-5) The Church is at its best when it recognizes its people and sends them into the world as ministers. Does your church recognize and celebrate your giftedness? How can your church help you be a better minister in your first, second, and third place?

- **GO:** (Acts 6:7) An awareness of our ministry in the world allows us to experience the Good News. Are you aware of your Christ-presence in the world? Will you follow Jesus out of the building and into the world?

Prayer
Lord, I want to be a minister in my home, at my work and in the world.

THE MINISTRY OF ALL CHRISTIANS
Day 32
"Bearing Fruit of Incarnational Ministry"

John 15:1-27 (NRSV)

[1]"I am the true vine, and my Father is the vinegrower. [2] He removes every branch in me that bears no fruit. Every branch that bears fruit he prunes to make it bear more fruit. [3]You have already been cleansed by the word that I have spoken to you. [4]Abide in me as I abide in you. Just as the branch cannot bear fruit by itself unless it abides in the vine, neither can you unless you abide in me. [5] I am the vine, you are the branches. Those who abide in me and I in them bear much fruit, because apart from me you can do nothing."

Matthew 25:34- (NRSV)

[34] "Then the king will say to those at his right hand, 'Come, you that are blessed by my Father, inherit the kingdom prepared for you from the foundation of the world; [35] for I was hungry and you gave me food, I was thirsty and you gave me something to drink, I was a stranger and you welcomed me, [36] I was naked and you gave me clothing, I was sick and you took care of me, I was in prison and you visited me.' [37] Then the righteous will answer him, 'Lord, when was it that we saw you hungry and gave you food, or thirsty and gave you something to drink? [38] And when was it that we saw you a stranger and welcomed you, or naked and gave you clothing? [39] And when was it that we saw you sick or in prison and visited you?' [40] And the king will answer them, 'Truly I tell you, just as you did it to one of the least of these who are members of my family, you did it to me.' "

———

Most churches in the United States would benefit from a good pruning. Much of our energy and many of our resources are being used to sustain practices, convictions, institutions and narratives that do not necessarily lead to the bearing of good fruit.
Philip D. Kenneson, *Life on the Vine*

Anyone who thinks sitting in church can make you a Christian must also think that sitting in a garage can make you a car.
Garrison Keillor

When you stop giving and offering something to the rest of the world, it's time to turn out the lights.
George Burns

One of Aesop's fables tells of a dying farmer who gathered his sons around his deathbed to tell them a secret. "My sons, I am shortly about to die. I would have you know that in my vineyard there lies a hidden treasure. Dig and you will find it." As soon as their father was dead, the sons took spades and began turning the vineyard soil in search of the treasure they thought was buried there. They never found the treasure, but all their thorough digging cultivated a crop like none before.

We had a garden when I was growing up. As a child, I wondered why the tomatoes, beans, corn, squash, and okra had a much harder time surviving than the weeds did, and often complained when Dad asked me to help get the weeds out.

———

If you want your vegetables to survive, you have to spend a great deal of time cultivating, fertilizing, pulling weeds, and hoeing. If you care about what is growing in your garden, the work has to be done. We are branches connected to Christ the vine. Likewise, by cultivating our connection to Christ, we will produce our best fruit.

A church I served held an annual block party in an effort to reach out to the surrounding community. At the first party in 2007, over 1200 people from the community joined us for an afternoon of fun, food, and music. A young boy who had lost both of his parents attended that year's party. He and his sister lived with their grandmother on the edge of poverty. The block party provided a wonderful outlet for those two young children as well as for many others. It also helped people in the community know that the "Church on the corner" cares.

A popular event at the party was the cakewalk. Church members made over one hundred cakes for the event. That young boy, nor his sister, had ever seen a homemade cake much less had one to eat. No one had ever baked him a cake for his birthday. He participated in the cakewalk and won, becoming the sole owner of a whole homemade cake! We fully expected him to take the cake home with him, enjoy it, and maybe share it with his sister and grandmother. Instead of keeping the cake for himself, he searched for his elementary school teacher who worshipped at the church. He wanted to give the cake to her because she had been nice to him and had helped him with his studies.

———

The fact that the young boy, who had never had a homemade cake, wanted to give his cake away speaks volumes about the impact of the block party, not only on the lives of those in the community but also for those in the church. And the King said, *for I was hungry and you gave me food, I was thirsty and you gave me something to drink, I was a stranger and you welcomed me, I was naked and you gave me clothing, I was sick and you took care of me, I was in prison and you visited me.*

Cultivate the Garden, Bear Fruit

- **WEED:** The scripture suggests that Jesus removes the branch that produces no fruit. What needs pruning or weeding from your life so you can be more fruitful in God's Kingdom work?

- **CULTIVATE**: What best practices (Bible study, prayer, worship, spiritual discipline, journaling, weekly communion) do you need to cultivate so you can be a producer of God's fruit?

- **BEAR FRUIT:** What difference did it make that the young boy won the cake at a church event where the Body of Christ was attempting to reach out to its community? How can you as an individual use your gifts to make a difference in someone else's life?

Prayer
Lord, help me to use my gifts to make a difference in your Kingdom.

———

NOTES:

The Ministry of All Christians

THE MINISTRY OF ALL CHRISTIANS
Day 33
"Created for God's Work"

Ephesians 2:8-10 (NRSV)
[8] For by grace you have been saved through faith, and this is not your own doing; it is the gift of God— [9] not the result of works, so that no one may boast. [10] For we are what he has made us, created in Christ Jesus for good works, which God prepared beforehand to be our way of life.

1 Thessalonians 1:3 (NIV)
We continually remember before our God and Father your work produced by faith, your labor prompted by love, and your endurance inspired by hope in our Lord Jesus Christ.

Genesis 1:26, 27 (RSV)
Then God said, "Let us make man in our own image…so God made man in his own image, in the image of God he created him; male and female, God created them.

> *The design of the gospel is this– that the image of God, which had been effaced by sin, may be stamped anew upon us, and that the advancement of this restoration may be continually going forward in us during our whole life, because God makes His glory shine forth in us by little and little.*
> John Calvin

> *Oz never did give nothin' to the Tin Man That he didn't, didn't already have*
> Dewey Bunnell

I remember one of the first songs I learned in Children's Choir. It goes like this:

> God made the sun up in the sky
> God made the lovely butterfly
> The smallest ant, the tallest tree
> And God made you, and God made me
> And God did something better still
> God gave us each our own free will
> And gave us each some work to do
> Some work for me, some work for you

The first thing the song celebrates is our createdness. We are created, not self-made. You are a signed original, with God's style, artistry, and vision all over you! The Psalmist reminds us, "It is God who has made us and not we, ourselves (Psalm 100:3)." We are created in the image of God. We carry in us the "imago Dei." Our createdness cannot be taken away, but it can be distorted and blurred by sin, the choices we make, and the persistence of our surrounding culture to remake us in its image. Createdness is not something that can be altered, only ignored, covered over, and forgotten; but our createdness is the bedrock of our identity.

Part of this God-image that defines us must surely be creativity. God's true power is creativity. God makes something, even everything, out of nothing. Now that's creativity! We need to shift our emphasis from God who overpowers to God who empowers, and from God's destructive might to God's constructive movement. This creative power, the ability to make possibility out of impossibility, will move us from fear to faith.

———

God creates us, Jesus calls us, and the Holy Spirit empowers us for co-creativity with the Holy. This co-creativity includes the use of all kinds of media: paint, clay, stone, wood, dance, food, even light – virtually everything that is made from the raw materials of the universe. We also create with ideas. Social structures, governments, faith communities, institutions, and movements are also artifacts of co-creation. Together we may co-create our preferred visions of the future. The best way to predict the future is to co-create it with God, in faithful Christ-community. This co-created future includes the future of our churches as missional, gifts-based, member-minister initiated embodiments of Christ's body.

The second half of the song declares that we all have work to do, even God's work to do. The Bible calls God's work "shalom." Shalom can be defined as the peace that prevails when all things work in their way for the good of the whole. This working is not about working our way to God or earning God's favor. It's about being and doing what we are created to be and to do. We are endowed with the spiritual gifts to do what we were created to do in the body of Christ. Ours is a purpose-given life. This purpose is to be about God's purposes.

In the book (and the movie based on the book), *The Help*, a child was told every day as part of a daily ritual with the family's maid, "You is beautiful. You is smart. You is important." In the Holy Book, we are told, "You are gifted. You are called. You are sent." You are endowed in your createdness in the image of God. You are called, by Jesus himself, to follow him and join him in his ongoing mission and ministry.

———

You are empowered by the same Holy Spirit that leads us all into life in the fullness of Christ. From his book, *Untamed*, Alan Hirsch asserts, "In the church that Jesus built, *everyone* gets to play! A person's conversion is their commission into ministry, and this is exactly the way Jesus designed his church to be. Disciples simply *are* ministers – they are created that way."

- **SAY TO YOURSELF,** "I am gifted. I am called. I am sent. I am endowed with spiritual gifts as part of my createdness in the image of God. I am called, by Jesus himself, to follow him and to join him in his ongoing mission and ministry. I am empowered by the Holy Spirit, who leads us all into life in the fullness of Christ."

- **FIND ANOTHER CHRIST-FOLLOWER AND SAY,** "You are gifted. You are called. You are sent. You are endowed with spiritual gifts as part of your createdness in the image of God. You are called, by Jesus himself, to follow him and join him in his ongoing mission and ministry. You are empowered by the Holy Spirit that leads us all into life in the fullness of Christ."

- **DISCERN YOUR CALL:** In what specific ways are you being called to co-create God's preferred vision for the world and all of its creatures? What "work of ministry" are you both endowed and called to do?

———

Prayer

Gracious God, help me embrace my createdness and the imago Dei *in me. Lead me into co-creativity with you, in partnership with Jesus and his Church, with the power of the Holy Spirit.*
Amen.

NOTES:

THE MINISTRY OF ALL CHRISTIANS
Day 34
"I Choose You"

John 15:15-17 (NRSV)

[15] I do not call you servants any longer, because the servant does not know what the master is doing; but I have called you friends, because I have made known to you everything that I have heard from my Father. [16] You did not choose me but I chose you. And I appointed you to go and bear fruit, fruit that will last, so that the Father will give you whatever you ask him in my name. [17] I am giving you these commands so that you may love one another.

"I have chosen you," Jesus said, "you have not chosen me." We are not our own; we have been bought with a price. Following Christ is not our initiative, merely our response, in obedience.
> Os Guinness

The truth, even though I cannot feel it right now, is that I am the chosen child of God, precious in God's eyes, called the Beloved from all eternity and held safe in an everlasting embrace...We must dare to opt consciously for our chosenness and not allow our emotions, feelings, or passions to seduce us into self-rejection."
> Henri J. M. Nouwen

But what I would like to say is that the spiritual life is a life in which you gradually learn to listen to a voice that says, "You are the beloved and on you my favor rests."...I want you to hear that voice. It is not a very loud voice because it is an intimate voice. It comes from a very deep place. It is soft and gentle. I want you to gradually hear that voice. We have to hear that voice and to claim for ourselves that that voice speaks the truth, our truth. It tells us who we are. That is where the spiritual life starts – by claiming the voice that calls us the beloved.

Henri J. M. Nouwen

We tend to grow into the names we are called and accept as true. Beautiful, awkward, graceful, talented, sneaky, or trustworthy – they tend to stick, even into adulthood. My mom called all of us kids "idgit" on a regular basis when we did things that she thought were careless or stupid. I guess the word is a hybrid of "fidgeting idiot." Sometimes I can hear her voice reinforcing the image of me as an "idgit." Sometimes, in spite of degrees, some measure of success (by the definition of my culture), and positions of responsibility, I hear and believe.

My church family called me gifted, beloved, forgiven, and called. The Psalmist reminds us that we are "wonderfully made" (Psalm 139:14) and that the original image of God in which we are created is pronounced by God to be "very good!" (Genesis 1:31).

It's a blessing to have faithful friends to help us choose the voices we can trust and the names into which we will grow. Most times, I hear and believe these voices.

Jesus says, "I call you my friends, not my servants. I call you by my name so you will be a servant to all, like me. I call you my friends." What does it mean to be a friend of Jesus? Jesus says it means we will do things his way, that we will do his commandments, and that we will do what he does. He expects that our friendship with him will shape all other friendships.

I wasn't the most athletic kid growing up. I got chosen last a lot. It feels good, it's affirming and empowering, when you are chosen to join a team or to be in a special group or to be part of an important mission. To hear the voice of Jesus say, "I choose you," is empowering, healing, and definitive. "I choose you to join my ongoing ministry of 'thy kingdom come,' on earth as it is in heaven."

All my life I heard that I must choose Jesus, to ask him to be my Lord and be the definitive relationship of my life; however the church, in an exercise of prevenient grace, didn't wait for me to choose to be part of the Body of Christ. They chose me. He chooses us to continue the incarnation, his Incarnation, Jesus in the flesh and blood of his disciples in every generation. I was encouraged to "choose my choosing," to willingly choose to follow Jesus who had already chosen me. I encourage you to do the same.

———

He calls us so that we can go bear fruit, spiritual fruit of love, joy, and peace, and tangible fruit of new disciples, justice, healing and wholeness for the "least among you." He calls all of us, not just designated ones of us. This means you, friend of Christ and co-minister with him and his church. The quote from Henri Nouwen uncovers the debilitating false humility that can rob us of true friendship with Jesus and allow us to talk ourselves out of our calling to join him in his ongoing ministry.

Listen to the very voice of Jesus say, "Remember, you did not choose me. I chose you."

- **TRY ON SOME BIBLICAL NAMES:**
  - Hear Jesus call you his "beloved." How does that feel?
  - What about the name "saint?" That's what the Apostle, Paul, calls us in Ephesians 4:12.

- **REMEMBER, YOU ARE CHOSEN BY CHRIST:** In what specific ways does the fact of being chosen by Jesus to be his friend and join him in his ongoing ministry affect your image of yourself and your place in the Church?

- **BE STILL** and cultivate the intimate, quiet relationship with Jesus until you hear him say, in your heart of hearts, "I choose you."

Prayer
Lord Jesus, lover of my soul, help me accept and embrace your choosing of me.
Amen.

———

THE MINISTRY OF ALL CHRISTIANS
Day 35
"Hearing God's Call"

1 Samuel 3:1-9 (RSV)

[1] Now the boy Samuel was ministering to the Lord under Eli. The word of the Lord was rare in those days; visions were not widespread. [2] At that time Eli, whose eyesight had begun to grow dim so that he could not see, was lying down in his room; [3] the lamp of God had not yet gone out, and Samuel was lying down in the temple of the Lord, where the ark of God was. [4] Then the Lord called, "Samuel! Samuel!" and he said, "Here I am!" [5] and ran to Eli, and said, "Here I am, for you called me." But he said, "I did not call; lie down again." So he went and lay down. [6] The Lord called again, "Samuel!" Samuel got up and went to Eli, and said, "Here I am, for you called me." But he said, "I did not call, my son; lie down again." [7] Now Samuel did not yet know the Lord, and the word of the Lord had not yet been revealed to him. [8] The Lord called Samuel again, a third time. And he got up and went to Eli, and said, "Here I am, for you called me." Then Eli perceived that the Lord was calling the boy. [9] Therefore Eli said to Samuel, "Go, lie down; and if he calls you, you shall say, "Speak, Lord, for your servant is listening.' " So Samuel went and lay down in his place.

> *Everybody has a vocation to some form of life-work. However, behind that call (and deeper than any call), everybody has a vocation to be a person to be fully and deeply human in Christ Jesus.*
> Brennan Manning

———

*I am not really very brave; I am not really
very strong; and I am not doing anything
spectacular. I am simply doing what God has
called me to do as a person who follows Him.
He said to feed His sheep and He said to care
for "the least of these," so that's what I'm
doing, with the help of a lot people who make
it possible and in the company of those who
make my life worth living.*
Katie J. Davis

The story of the call of Samuel is not only a story about one person's experience, it offers a gift bag of handles for understanding the dynamics of God's call on our lives. The writer explains that "the word of God was rare in those days and there was no frequent vision." Some may say that there are too many voices identifying themselves as God's true messengers and their word is the real "word of God." Maybe there are too many "visions" out there competing for our attention and our loyalty. It's helpful to find someone or some community to help us discern the wisdom and will of God.

Samuel was literally raised in the temple under the mentorship of the priest, Eli. He knew all about the Jewish faith, the rituals, the meaning of symbols, all the stories and teachings from the Torah and God's commandments. Yet, we are told, he does not yet know the Lord, and God's call had not been revealed to him. Like Samuel, we may have varying degrees of personal church history, growing up with at least some exposure to the Gospel and church culture. We may know *about* God without any sense of knowing God or of God knowing us in some personal way.

———

It's a great blessing to have people in our lives who love us into the love of God, who know us and love us even before we know the love of God in any personal, formative and transformative way.

Samuel is being called for God's purposes in a very direct way, when Eli finally gets the message and guides Samuel to hear and respond to that call. Everybody needs an Eli or an Eliza to help them distinguish the voice of God from many other voices, to hear the call of Jesus, and prepare us to respond. Sometimes we need someone to tell us, "Pay attention to that. That's a God thing."

We tend to use the word "vocation" to describe a person's career or profession. It literally means "calling." In the best of situations, a people will feel a deep sense of purpose in what they spend their lives doing, a sense of calling. More than working to make a living, vocation is about living with a purpose beyond our selves. Vocation is life's call, life's work. It's called your "life's work" because it will take your whole life to do it! You may take a vacation from your career, but not from your life's work. It finds it's way into every conversation, every decision, and every relationship.

God had been calling Samuel, even before that definitive night, calling Samuel into a life of spirit-gifted service. God is calling all of us, continually, toward our vocation, the work of our lives. We are called on many levels: God calls us into being, into relationship with him, and into a life of service as disciples of Jesus Christ according to our gifting and our circumstances.

———

Sometimes we are "called" or summoned into action by the circumstances that arise around us. In a cruciform pattern, we find ourselves at the intersection of perceived need and our response-ability. It's an "ah-ha" moment when we realize that the "someone" in "someone ought to do something" is us!

Instead of waiting to be called by a member of the ministry staff, tune your heart to the call of Jesus. Ministry staff and fellow member-ministers can help you hear and respond to the call of Jesus on your life, but it's your call.

- **ASK:** Ask others who seem to have a clear sense of call to tell you their call story. How did they come to "hear" their call? Did anyone help them sort it out? What are they doing in response to that call?

- **RECALL:** Have you ever had a sense of calling? How did it come about? What are you doing in response to it?
    - Who have helped you hear and respond to the call of God in your life? If you haven't already, seek them out and thank them.

- **IMAGINE:** Picture a congregation in which no person's calling from Jesus was ranked any higher or more special or holy than anyone else's – not the pastor's, nor the ministry staff's, nor the Sunday school teacher's nor the mission trip leader's. What if all Jesus' followers realize that they are called into "fulltime Christian service" and that their calling is as valid and holy as any professional Christian's? What new forms of ministry could break out in a congregation of called people?

- **LISTEN:** What about you? How are you being called to serve Christ as part of his body?

Prayer

Lord Jesus, make my ears attentive to your voice and my spirit eager to respond, that having heard you speak, I may have some part, in partnership with you, in answering someone else's prayers.
Amen.

NOTES:

THE MINISTRY OF ALL CHRISTIANS
Day 36
"You are a Priest in the Priesthood of All Believers"

1 Peter 2:9-10 (NRSV)
[9] But you are a chosen people, a royal priesthood, a holy nation, God's special possession, that you may declare the praises of him who called you out of darkness into his wonderful light. [10] Once you were not a people, but now you are the people of God; once you had not received mercy, but now you have received mercy.

> *Let everyone, therefore, who knows himself to be a Christian be assured of this, and apply it to [themselves] – that we are all priests, and there is no difference between us.*
> Martin Luther

> *The priesthood of all believers, therefore, does not only mean that each person is his or her [own] priest...In very personal terms, it means that the "minister" is your priest and that you are the minister's priest; that you are my priest and I am your priest; that we are God's representatives to each other, and we are each other's representatives before God. It means that we are to speak to each other about God, calling each other to repentance and faith. It means that we are to speak to God about each other, interceding before God for each other, and seeking God's guidance and blessing.*
> Greg Ogden, *Unfinished Business*[5]

Your conversion is your commission; your baptism is your ordination.
Alan Hirsch

I remember the first Thanksgiving dinner with the new extended family that I had married into. After a full day of cooking and arranging for extra places for people to sit down and eat, our family gathered around the dinner table and awkwardly looked around. There was sense that we were waiting for something to happen but no one would say it. We joined hands and bowed our heads…and waited. I looked up with one eye and caught my new cousin-in-law peeking with one of her eyes. That started us to giggling and soon the house was full of laughter. Finally my mother-in-law said, "Chris, you're supposed to pray!" I said something like, ""Really? Why me?" And she explained, "Well, you're the only preacher in the family, so you're supposed to pray." To that I said, "I guess that makes me the DRP – the designated religious person." I went along in order to get along because we were hungry and the food was getting cold, but I knew that there were a lot of Christian disciples in my extended family and that any of them, including the children, could have offered thanks to God for our food and our family on that day.

Saint Peter declares that the Church, the body of Jesus followers, is a "holy nation" – like Israel, a community of faith called to embody the Gospel, life in the fullness of Christ, a beacon to the world, a living example of God's kingdom coming "on earth as it is in heaven."

———

He calls us a "priesthood of all believers." By his definition, we are priests, to each other and to others in the name of Christ. We are called *as a group*, in addition to our individual calling, to be a priestly presence in the world, in the communities in which we live, play, and work, raise our children, shop and serve.

So, what do priest do? First, they are open to God's calling to serve. They prepare themselves for the works of ministry for which they are gifted by God. By definition, priests help lead worship. They offer prayers on behalf of others and commend them to God. They usher others into the presence of God. By that, I mean that they help connect people with the God who already knows and loves them. Priests act as "go betweens" when they intercede on behalf of others, literally getting between them and their difficulties. As priests, we not only offer prayers of intercession, but we offer ourselves as a bridge or a buffer in the midst of people's suffering.

John Wesley calls the ways God's grace is channeled to us (like water through a hose) or the ways we can know and experience God's grace "means of grace." These means of grace include the sacraments of communion and baptism, worship and prayer, acts of mercy, and spiritual disciplines like Bible reading and fasting. As part of the priesthood of all believers, we are blessed to become means of grace ourselves, conveying God's grace to others.

———

I remember when the members of my church, my faith family, a priesthood of believers, placed their hands on my head and prayed for my healing at the death of my mother. I remember when members of the priesthood of all believers made the sign of the cross on my forehead with water and invited me to remember my baptism and be thankful. I remember with thanksgiving how Sunday school teachers and youth group mentors taught me to know and to love God's word. I remember when everyday Christians acted as my priests, praying that the Holy Spirit would empower me to repent of my sins and live a new life of greater faithfulness.

My friend Ed and I were talking about a church in which everyone was a minister of some sort, and every member was a priest at some time. He was puzzled and asked, "Who will be their pastor?" and I replied, before I could think about it and talk myself out of it, "We'll take turns."

- **PONDER**: How does it feel to think of yourself as a "priest?"

- **CLAIM THE NAME:** Receive and embrace the name of "priest" - not because you would think to call yourself that, but because the biblical writers call you that, in the name and for the sake of the ministry of Jesus, the ministry of all Christians.

- **PREPARE YOURSELF:** Get ready to lead others in worship by your worship; teach others the scriptures by being a co-learner, and offer your self in everyday interactions as a means of grace to others.

———

- **DO PROESTLY THINGS FOR OTHERS:**
  Pray with and for others; share life wisdom
  from the Holy Scriptures in your own words
  and from your own experiences; be a vessel
  for the presence of Jesus as you meet with,
  converse with, and interact with one or more
  other person. (Remember, Jesus promises,
  "When two or more are gathered in my name,
  I will be there in the midst of you."). Rather
  than offering ritual sacrifices at the altar, be a
  living sacrifice, laying down your life for the
  sake of others in Jesus' name, after his
  example.

Prayer

*Lord Jesus, help me overcome my uneasiness about
being a "minister" or a "priest" because of the way I
have understood those roles in the church. Help me
embrace and humbly prepare for my calling as a
priest in the priesthood of all believers and the
ministry of all Christians, because it is your ministry
to which I am called.*
Amen.

NOTES:

THE MINISTRY OF ALL CHRISTIANS
Day 37
"Engage your Gifts"

Matthew 21:28-31 (NRSV)

[28] "What do you think? A man had two sons; he went to the first and said, 'Son, go and work in the vineyard today.' [29] He answered, 'I will not'; but later he changed his mind and went. [30] The father went to the second and said the same; and he answered, 'I go, sir'; but he did not go. [31] Which of the two did the will of his father?"

> *Perhaps the greatest single weakness of the contemporary Christian Church is that millions of supposed members are not really involved at all and, what is worse, do not think it strange that they are not. As soon as we recognize Christ's intention to make His Church a militant company we understand at once that the conventional arrangement cannot suffice. There is no real chance of victory in a campaign if 90 percent of the soldiers are untrained and uninvolved, but that is exactly where we stand now.*
> Elton Trueblood

I am equipped for playing golf. I have a complete set of clubs in my car, each club designed for a different kind of golfing challenge. I have specially equipped shoes and every golfing gadget known to humankind. I have a golfing glove and several kinds of tees. I have divot fixer and cool little coins to mark my place on the putting green. I am equipped all right. Trouble is, I seldom play. I don't play enough to call myself a golfer, unless watching other people play counts.

———

The same could be said for the vast majority of Christian believers and church members. Only about 35% of registered church members are active in any way in the life and ministry of their home congregations. That's the average for mainline denominational churches in the United States. Even fewer are engaged in ministries to others outside the walls of the church. Yours may vary some depending on how old your congregation is. The older the congregation, the more dramatic becomes the gap between active and inactive. And, most congregations seem to be "OK" with that. When I quote those statistics at church meetings and training sessions, people say, "That sounds pretty good to me," or, "Wow, that's better than I expected."

When people join most any congregation or faith community, they make promises of deeper discipleship and commitments of their prayers, presence, gifts, service, and witness in support of the ministries of the Church and the kingdom work of Jesus. Isn't it strange to make a vow of presence and then be so absent? The gifts of God, given for the continuing work of Jesus in his "kingdom come" ministry, cannot be engaged if those who are endowed with those gifts are missing in action. They remind me of the second son in the parable from the text above. They said they would do the work of Christ, but didn't. Thank God, there is grace, and we can change our mind the other way and reengage the promises we have made.

What about those who are "present and accounted for?" Are we all engaging the gifts we have been given?

———

As several folks have responded to the introduction of "equipping ministry" language into our congregational culture, "We are already equipped!" How true, but how many of those gifts are being engaged for doing the work of Christ as part of an outward-focused, missional church?

In the years since its beginning, the Christian movement has become more institutionalized and inward-focused and less movemental and outward-focused. Certainly in the years since WWII, the Church has developed more of a membership culture than a discipleship culture. We have forgotten that the Church exists primarily for those who are not in it. Over time, the Church has organized itself for the care of its members, not for outreach, incarnational mission, and evangelism. The core missional emphases of Ephesians 4 – apostleship, prophecy, evangelism, shepherding, and teaching – have been largely reduced to the last two, pastors and lay folk focused on taking care of a local flock and teaching and preaching for personal edification and spiritual self-satisfaction.

Of course, we need to tend to the core processes of worship, study, and taking care of one another in Christian love. If the love of Christ does not move us out to know, and to love, and to care for "the least of these;" it is of no value and devotion becomes an end in itself. In outward-focused equipping churches, believers are activated as missioners and evangelists. The spiritual equipment with which we are endowed is activated for incarnational ministry, the ministry of all and of each Christian.

———

You may have heard of the "80:20 Rule. [See the meditation for "Day 1"] It states that in most volunteer organizations 20 percent of the people do 80 percent of the work. As the Church, we do not belong to a volunteer organization. We are not volunteers. We are disciples. We are "membered" into the very Body of Christ to embody him in service to others. Elton Trueblood's ratio for the Church, quoted above, is 90:10. It exposes the fact that only 10 percent of the members of most congregations are active as disciples of Christ, as ministers of the Gospel, providing leadership in the congregation and doing the work of Christ out in the world. Equipping ministry, as an expression of active discipleship within a congregational culture, seeks to flip that number. It seeks to engage spiritual gifts and Holy Spirit power to enact those other three promises in addition to prayers and presence – gifts, service, and witness; to reinterpret those first two to include the willingness to cooperate with God and embody Jesus as an instrument for the answering of some of those prayers and being present in person with others away from the church property.

- **CHECK YOUR PRAYER CLOSET** for rusty unused spiritual equipment. It's there, implanted in you. Get it out and take it out into the world for some practice shots. The Holy Spirit promises to make it "like riding a bike." Pretty soon you'll be ministering like a pro!

- **HELP "FLIP THIS HOUSE":** Like the popular show on the A&E channel, help your housemates in the household of God flip the congregation's missional engagement ratio from 65 percent inactive to 100 percent active. Become an equipping ministry evangelist. Encourage and enlist others into active engagement in the ongoing ministry and mission of Jesus.

Prayer

Lord Jesus, I confess that I have spiritual gifts for ministry that I am not engaging for your sake. Show me anew how I may serve you by serving others.

―――

NOTES:

THE MINISTRY OF ALL CHRISTIANS
Day 38
"Aligned for Ministry"

Ephesians 4:11-13 (NRSV)
[11]The gifts he gave were that some would be apostles, some prophets, some evangelists, some pastors and teachers, [12]to equip the saints for the work of ministry, for building up the body of Christ, [13]until all of us come to the unity of the faith and of the knowledge of the Son of God, to maturity, to the measure of the full stature of Christ.

Romans 12:4-8 (NRSV)
[4]For as in one body we have many members, and not all the members have the same function, [5]so we, who are many, are one body in Christ, and individually we are members one of another. [6]We have gifts that differ according to the grace given to us: prophecy, in proportion to faith; [7]ministry, in ministering; the teacher, in teaching; [8]the exhorter, in exhortation; the giver, in generosity; the leader, in diligence; the compassionate, in cheerfulness.

> *Beauty is finding the right fit, the natural fit.*
> *Avoid trying to be someone you're not.*
> Rick Riordan

> *Don't try to fit in when you are supposed to*
> *stand out and don't try to stand out when you*
> *are supposed to fit it. When you are trying too*
> *hard, then you are doing the wrong thing.*
> Joseph Cubby

There's a world of difference between being "good tired" and "bad tired." You've probably been both in your life. You know how it is to do something because you feel you ought to do it or simply because someone asked for your help. Sometimes we call this "getting volunteered." It may even be a task that is part of a mission that you believe in. You can do it. You labor long and hard. At the end of the day you are worn out and drained, and you tell yourself, "I sure don't want to do that again." That's "bad tired."

I hope you've had the opposite experience. Your heart and your imagination are captured by a sense of mission or of hope. You labor long and hard, but it doesn't feel like work. Not only are you able to do it, you are compelled, inspired, and determined to do it. You'd do it "like it's your job," as a young friend puts it) but you'd do it for free. You'd do it even if it cost you something. At the end of the day you are worn out yet exhilarated. And you tell yourself, "I can't wait to get back at it!" That's "good tired."

One key to being "good tired" is serving in and through, or more precisely *as* the Church, whether it is in the more internal life of the congregation - management of its resources, the care of its members, and the traditions of worship and disciple formation – or in its outreach as a missional movement into the community. The Bible describes this as never becoming weary of well doing. A key to the possibility of being "good tired" is being in a capacity and in a setting that are a "good fit" ministry.

Members who are engaged in some form of congregational or missional service often find themselves "bad tired" after serving in multiple places where their gifts and passions for ministry just don't fit the tasks and roles they are given. Yes, there are plenty of examples in the Bible of people who didn't feel suited or gifted to do the work to which God called them. You may be one of those whom God calls to do something that seems totally unlikely, but in moving forward in faith, God will be faithful to equip and empower.

In deference to biblical stories of unlikely people called to do mighty deeds for God, we may be tempted to overlook or undervalue the more pervasive pattern of ministry according to spiritual gifting and the activation of what we already have and are in the service of Christ, the church, and our neighbors. More the rule than the exception, God calls us to engage our spiritual gifting and createdness for the work of ministry, even the ongoing ministry of Jesus in the world. The process of ministry matching involves more than connecting the dots from a "Spiritual Gifts Inventory" to a list of service opportunities in a catalog of ministry descriptions.

Yes, we are all endowed with spiritual gifts for ministry. Taking a spiritual gifts inventory is a helpful part of the process of connecting the dots, but there's more. There are things that you see around you that make you righteously angry or that hook your heart with palpable compassion. There are people and causes that make your heart beat in rhythm with the heart of Christ. These heartbeats are a clue to your ministry calling.

———

You have a personality that forms the lenses through which you see the world and preconditions the ways you respond to people and tasks. God wants to use your unique personhood, in partnership with others knit together in the Body of Christ, to do the work of Christ.

When your car is out of alignment, it wears out the tires, strains the steering system, and shakes the body. When our serving is out of alignment with our gifting, passion, and abilities, it wears us out, keeps us moving in the wrong direction, and tears up the Body of Christ. When we find our fit, we'll fit more perfectly together, and together we'll move toward the fullness of Christ and his preferred vision for the world that he "so loves."

- **TAKE A SPIRITUAL GIFTS INVENTORY:** If you haven't already, take a spiritual gifts discovery inventory. If you have done this recently, retouch the results. Do others see those gifts in you? Are you serving in alignment with those gifts?

- **REENGAGE YOUR PASSIONATE PASTIMES:** Make a quick list of three things you enjoy doing. When was the last time you did them?

- **WITNESS:** Tell a friend a story of a time when you were "good tired."

- **GET AN ALIGNMENT:** Take a second look at the ways you are serving Christ as part of

———

his body, the church. How does your serving align with your gifting, passion, and abilities?

Prayer

Lord, grant me the courage to discover the gifts for ministry that you have implanted in me, and the joy of engaging them for the works of ministry to which Jesus calls me.
Amen.

———

NOTES:

THE MINISTRY OF ALL CHRISTIANS
Day 39
"Doing the Things that Jesus Does"

John 14:12 (NRSV)

[12] Very truly, I tell you, the one who believes in me will also do the works that I do and, in fact, will do greater works than these, because I am going to the Father.

> *Action is always superior to speech in the Gospels, which is why the Word became flesh and not newsprint.*
> Colin M. Morris, *Mankind My Church*

When the teachers, prophets, and poets of the Bible use the word "you," they are speaking to at least two "yous." One is the person or group of people they were addressing at the time, such as when God says to Abraham, "I will be your God and you will be my people." Or, when Paul says to his protégé in ministry, Timothy, "Do not let anyone think less of you because you are young, but set the believers an example."

The other is to you and me and anyone who reads or hears the words of scripture in personal times of devotion or in public services of worship or Bible study. In God's word to Abraham, God is saying to us, both as the Church and as individual disciples, "I will be your God and you will be my people." In his word to Timothy, Paul is encouraging readers in every generation to take courage from their calling and the strength of the Holy Spirit to live faithfully and to be an example of deep discipleship.

———

When Jesus says, "You will do the things I do…" he is speaking to his beloved first group of disciples. It was a moment of awesome awakening when my mentors in the faith helped me hear Jesus saying to me as a young person of 12 years old, "You, yes you, will do the things I do." It was an unmistakable call to follow him and partner with him in his ongoing works of ministry – not necessarily as an ordained pastor, but as his disciple.

He is speaking to us as the Church and to us as present-day disciples. He is calling us to lives of ministry, in his name and as his body. In fact, he says we will do greater things than he because he is going to the Father and pouring out his Spirit, releasing ministry from one time and place to all times and all places. Greater things? Wow! How about starting with doing the things he does:

- Loving without condition
- Feeding
- Healing
- Clothing
- Welcoming
- Offering life-giving water
- Teaching about God's vision for the world
- Confronting unjust powers
- Saving others from all manner of death-dealing circumstances
- Laying down his life for the sake of others
- Exposing religious pride
- Visiting the sick and imprisoned
- Praying, alone and in groups
- Reading and embodying God's word in scripture

In his book *Mere Christianity*, C. S. Lewis asserts that the Church "exists for nothing else but to draw [people] into Christ, to make them little Christs. If they are not doing that, all the cathedrals, clergy, missions, sermons, even the Bible itself, are simply a waste of time. God became Man for no other purpose… Every Christian is to become a little Christ. The whole purpose of becoming a Christian is simply nothing else."[6] We may demure and insist that we are not Christ, but Christ says we are his very body and we will do the things he does. As we participate in services of Holy Communion, we pray that we may become more like Christ:

> Grant us, therefore, gracious Lord, so
> to partake of this Sacrament of thy Son
> Jesus Christ, that we may walk in
> newness of life, may grow into his
> likeness, and may evermore dwell in
> him, and he in us. Amen.

Martin Luther, in his tract *The Freedom of a Christian* (1520), writes "[A]s our heavenly Father has in Christ freely come to our aid, we also ought freely to help our neighbor through our body and its works, and each one should become as it were a Christ to the other that we may be Christs to one another and Christ may be the same in all, that is, that we may be truly Christians…"[7]

---

[6] C.S. Lewis, *Mere Christianity*, © 1952 and 1980, *The Complete C.S. Lewis, Signature Classics*, HarperCollins Publishers, © 2002, C.S. Lewis Pte. Ltd., p. 144.

[7] http://aardvarkalley.blogspot.com/2007/02/martin-luther-doctor-and-reformer.html

Remember Jesus assures us, "You will do the things I do."

You don't start out doing all of this all at once or at a high level of confidence or competence. Remember, Jesus promises helpmates that include the Holy Spirit and each other in our communities of faith. He promises to be with us always. Remember that we are in a lifelong process of growing into his likeness as we cooperate with the Holy Spirit and go about our apprenticeship to Jesus with passion and purpose, with aspiration and intention. Not everyone will be called upon to fill the same roles or do the same "Jesus things." There are many gifts and many ways of service. We are one body, after all, with many parts.[8]

- **TAKE AN INVENTORY:** From the list of the things Jesus does, what things are you already doing in some way in your family, our church, your neighborhood, your friendships, and your places of work, recreation, and community involvement?

- **REMEMBER AND THANK** someone who has been "Christ for you" in some way. If possible, do it face-to-face.

- **ASK AND DO:** What "Jesus things" could you, with the help of the Holy Spirit and friends in faith, begin doing?

---

[8] 1 Corinthians 12:12-27

Prayer

Free me from being so heavenly minded that I am no earthly good, from holding you so high that it releases me from any responsibility, telling myself that I could never do the things you did and continue to do.

———

NOTES:

THE MINISTRY OF ALL CHRISTIANS
Day 40
"Go!"

Matthew 28:18b-20 (NRSV)
[18b] All authority in heaven and on earth has been given to me. [19] Go therefore and make disciples of all nations, baptizing them in the name of the Father and of the Son and of the Holy Spirit, [20] and teaching them to obey everything that I have commanded you. And remember, I am with you always, to the end of the age.'

Isaiah 6:8 (NRSV)
Then I heard the voice of the Lord saying, "Whom shall I send, and who will go for us?" And I said, "Here am I; send me!"

> *God did not direct His call [exclusively] to Isaiah— Isaiah overheard God saying, "...who will go for Us?" The call of God is not just for a select few but for everyone. Whether I hear God's call or not depends on the condition of my ears, and exactly what I hear depends upon my spiritual attitude.*
> Oswald Chambers

> *The mark of a great church is not its seating capacity, but its sending capacity.*
> Mike Stachura

> *Missions is not the 'ministry of choice' for a few hyperactive Christians in the church. Missions is the purpose of the church.*
> Unknown

———

I remember one of my first experiences of doing church away from our church property. It happened when our 6th grade Sunday school teacher suggested that we take our Vacation Bible School on the road and set up in a neighborhood not far from our church. It was a neighborhood that my parents had warned me about. I wasn't to walk through it and we rarely drove through it as a family. It was filled with people who looked different from me who lived closer together and in less nice homes than most of my friends did. Nevertheless we partnered with some families that she knew and did Bible School on their front lawns and porches.

It was an unforgettable week. We made friends and were joined at the heart, even the heart of Jesus. I realize now that our teacher was responding to a call from Jesus to leave the comfort and familiarity of our church campus and to join Jesus in his ministry to people "out there."

Wouldn't it be great if we had a vast missionary service deployed across our towns and cities? Well, we do! Among the many statements of faith in our hymnals and books of worship is one called "A Modern Affirmation." It begins with this declaration: "Where the Spirit of the Lord is, there is the one true church, apostolic and universal...." Where is the church located? Can you Google the address? No. Where the Holy Spirit is active in God's people acting as Jesus, incarnating Christ, there is the Church.

The Church is Holy-Spirited people acting at the prodding of the Spirit, working in the Spirit. If we are the Church, are we the Church when we are not at the church? If we are the Church, individually and corporately, and we are in neighborhoods, stores, places of business and recreation, then the Church is there. We are that vast missionary corps!

Jesus clearly says, "Go." He doesn't say, "Stay where you are and get people to come to you." He says, "Come out here. Join me where I am." There is such a thing as being "over-churched." We simply can't stay at the church doing churchy things with churchy people if we are to follow Jesus.

Consider this benediction from Leonard Sweet's book, *So Beautiful - Divine Design for Life and the Church* (page 60). Someday I'll get up the nerve to use it after worship at our church:

> *"Want to follow Jesus? Leave the church. Get **out** of the church. Leave. I mean it. Right now. Get **out** of here. Scram. Now. Out of here. Did you hear me? Leave this church. **Now!** Jesus says, 'Go Do Me.' Go be Jesus."*

LOOK AROUND: Where is the Spirit of the Lord moving? What are the needs around you that are calling you out of the church building and into the world, the neighborhood, and the hangouts inhabited by people Jesus loves, but who may not know it or who may have a need Jesus needs you to help him meet?

―――

ASK YOURSELF: Am I either over churched or under utilized in the hands of God, as the hands of Jesus? What is something, someone, or group of someones that would help solve both problems at the same time?

GO: When you find the answer, or even as you look for an answer to the last question, take steps in that direction. Take some people with you. Sometimes you are better served to be still and wait on the Lord. Sometimes it's better to make a move in the direction of those whom Jesus loves and find him there.

Prayer
Lord Jesus, help me go where you lead and be faithful when I'd rather stay where I'm accustomed to being taught, inspired, and fed.

About the writers

Matthew Burton provides overall pastoral leadership for Clemmons United Methodist Church in Clemmons, North Carolina where he continues to cast the vision for a church that equips and then releases God's people into mission and ministry. His doctoral work at United Theological Seminary in Dayton, Ohio focused on "Casting the Vision: An Equipping Ministry Launch for a Gift-Based Lay Ministry." **burtonm@clemmonsumc.org**

Chris B. Hughes and his wife Gloria serve at Clemmons United Methodist Church in Clemmons, North Carolina providing leadership in equipping ministry and discipleship. Chris did his doctor of ministry work at Drew University in the area of pastoral leadership with a focus on "Co-Creating the Church of the FuturePresent." He is heavily invested in the church's processes of making disciples, especially in the enterprise of Confirmation. **www.chrisbhughes.net**

———

Elizabeth Wourms is the Executive Pastor at the Dayton Vineyard Church, Dayton Ohio. Elizabeth played a key role in launching Kingdom Connections of Greater Dayton, a faith-based non-profit organization committed to community transformation. Her past ministry experience includes serving as the Involvement Pastor of Beavercreek Church of the Nazarene and Director of the Pohly Center for Supervision and Leadership Formation at United Theological Seminary where she completed her doctor of ministry degree.
ewourms@att.net

R. Robert Creech is Professor of Christian Ministries and Director of Pastoral Ministries at the Truett Theological Seminary, Baylor University. Before joining the Truett faculty Robert served for 22 years as Senior Pastor at the University Baptist Church in Houston, Texas. He had previously taught on the faculty of Houston Baptist University. Robert earned his Ph.D. from Baylor University in New Testament studies. He co-authored *The Leader's Journey* and has published chapters in several other volumes.
Robert_Creech@baylor.edu

Dennis Ammons – Cover photos and design

21761457R00112

Made in the USA
Lexington, KY
28 March 2013